June 30, 91

D0170190

Laura,

Have read of your exploits. Continue in faith, hope and assurance — the seed will grow (Mk 4:26-29).

George

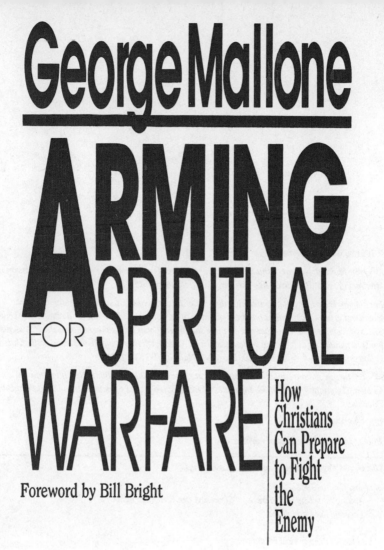

George Mallone

ARMING FOR SPIRITUAL WARFARE

How
Christians
Can Prepare
to Fight
the
Enemy

Foreword by Bill Bright

INTERVARSITY PRESS
DOWNERS GROVE, ILLINOIS 60515

© 1991 by George Mallone

All rights reserved. No part of this book may be reproduced in any form without written permission from InterVarsity Press, P.O. Box 1400, Downers Grove, Illinois 60515.

InterVarsity Press is the book-publishing division of InterVarsity Christian Fellowship, a student movement active on campus at hundreds of universities, colleges and schools of nursing in the United States of America, and a member movement of the International Fellowship of Evangelical Students. For information about local and regional activities, write Public Relations Dept., InterVarsity Christian Fellowship, 6400 Schroeder Rd., P.O. Box 7895, Madison, WI 53707-7895.

All Scripture quotations, unless otherwise indicated, are from the Holy Bible, New International Version. Copyright © 1973, 1978, International Bible Society. Used by permission of Zondervan Bible Publishers.

ISBN 0-8308-1734-4

Printed in the United States of America ∞

Library of Congress Cataloging-in-Publication Data

Mallone, George, 1944-
    Arming for spiritual warfare: how Christians can prepare to fight
the enemy/George Mallone.
      p.   cm.
Includes bibliographical references.
ISBN 0-8308-1734-4
1. Spiritual life—Pentecostal authors. 2. Suffering—Religious
aspects—Christianity. 3. Persecution. 4. Temptation. 5. Devil—
Controversial literature. 6. Church growth. 7. Kingdom of God.
8. Mallone, George, 1944-   . I. Title. II. Title: Spiritual
warfare.
BV4501.2.M332   1990
248.4'8994—dc20   90-46663
                                    CIP

15	14	13	12	11	10	9	8	7	6	5	4	3	2	1
02	01	00	99	98	97	96	95	94	93	92	91			

To Bonnie:
God's queen,
mighty warrior,
my hero.

Foreword

During the past thirty-nine years of worldwide ministry for our dear Lord, I have graciously been allowed by God to witness great spiritual victories in every corner of the globe. Tens of millions of people are coming to Christ as the message of God's love and forgiveness is sweeping the world in unprecedented ways. We are seeing the moving of God's Spirit as never before, from the miraculous fall of the Berlin Wall to the opening of spiritual doors in Eastern Europe and the Soviet Union—doors that have been closed for decades.

But just as we are witnesses to this great and mighty moving of God's Spirit, we are also seeing the evidence of intensified spiritual warfare. The enemy is seemingly mobilizing massive forces to counterattack the working of God throughout the world.

Never before have I seen such demonstration of monumental spiritual battle, from the tragic moral decay and godlessness of the West, to the terrible grip of false religions and ideologies that have captured the minds and hearts of millions in nation after nation.

In *Arming for Spiritual Warfare,* George Mallone addresses the subject of spiritual warfare in a practical, challenging way. He has explored a difficult subject from a thorough, careful study of Scripture with a real eye toward the ways in which Satan wages war on believers both in large issues and in small, everyday matters.

But although this book helps us to recognize Satan and his tactics, the focus throughout is clearly on Jesus Christ as our source and power for spiritual victory. As you read this book, you will rejoice with me that though we are in spiritual battle daily, even moment by moment, George Mallone has reminded us that our victory is in the power and might of Jesus Christ, our Overcomer, King of kings and Lord of lords.

Bill Bright
President
Campus Crusade for Christ

Preface

When I began this project in April 1989, I felt the burden of incredible pain and opposition. Bonnie, my wife of over twenty years, was suffering with her third bout of cancer. Her life seemed to be hanging by the power of persistent prayer and a sovereign God. The whole family suffered: my children were struggling with the possibility of life without Mom, and I found myself moping about the house, wondering how I would have the strength to live.

This was also a time when we were facing the daily pressures of planting a new church in Arlington, Texas. It was hard enough to be facing the spiritual opposition one would expect with such a task. But what made that time even worse was that it was a season in which evil was spoken about me—even by those I considered friends.

In those months I felt Job-like. It seemed the hedge had been pulled back and the demons of hell were ravaging my life.

You may be wondering why a man, given my position at the time, would want to write a book on spiritual warfare. After all, wouldn't writing a book like this only invite more wrath from the devil? There are two main reasons I decided to write.

First, I received a prophetic word from the Lord about writing this book, and I wanted to be obedient. I believe God still gives specific revelation to specific people at specific times. A prophetic word does not override the integrity and wisdom of the person receiving the revelation. Likewise it must not violate nor add to Scripture, but confirm it.

This prophetic word came from a friend who called from Canada in early January 1989. I have known Terry for years, and I've come to trust his perception of God's voice. After a friendly chat I asked Terry, "Has the Lord said anything to you about me?"

"Just one word," he said. "Write the book!" Unbeknownst to Terry, a contract for this book had been sitting on my desk for four months, with a reply due in January.

My second reason for writing is more personal. I am tired of catching the enemy's flack. Bonnie and I have been under siege, and now we want to expose the enemy's schemes to God's light, and defeat as many of his plans as we can. We want to take back territory, and we want you to take it back with us.

We all need to be armed for spiritual warfare. In this book, I want to show how Christians can prepare to fight the enemy. First, I want to *expose* some of the schemes of the enemy, to pull back the curtain on his devastating and cunning ways. I then want to *equip* us to wield the sword of the Spirit. And thirdly, I want to *enlist* soldiers in the fight.

Unfortunately, many Christians have little idea that a war is even going on—let alone on what fronts it's being fought and with what weapons. Soldiers are evaluated by how they do in battle, not by the uniforms they wear or the titles they carry. We want to be ready to take the offensive with the enemy as we fight to take ground for God.

There's nothing easy about being a warrior in God's army. For those who think it's making great warriors out of Bonnie and me, my response is somewhat like Winston Churchill's after the defeat of his conservative government: " 'Winston,' said his wife, 'it may well be a blessing in disguise.' 'At the moment,' replied Churchill, 'it seems quite effectively disguised.' "

There will be casualties in this war. The best advice in the world and the most persistent prayers cannot change this fact. There is no need to feel guilty about what we have not known or done in the past. Today, we will learn to fight—and we'll leave the conclusion of the war to our General.

A number of books have been written on spiritual warfare in the last decade. Gone are the days when we relied exclusively upon Jessie Penn-Lewis's *War on the Saints* to address the theme for us.[1]

However, a mistaken and unbiblical trend toward dualism is developing in today's literature on spiritual warfare. Instead of producing faith in God's overcoming ability, some works instill fear. The Bible views Satan as a weak shadowy figure, who stays in the background whenever God is doing his glorious work—not as one who has an equal amount of power. Satan is no match for God. We are to give him no glory by fearing his works or power.

In this book, I want to instill faith that Satan is "God's devil."[2] He is a hooked fish which has been hauled into the boat. He flops madly in his last bid for life, but is doomed to die. We need to be careful not to get too close as he fights, but he is grounded and his doom is sure.

As my writing for this book ends, our fight continues as Bonnie recovers from her fourth cancer surgery. Although I am more encouraged, there are still moments when the pressure is overwhelming. Yet God has sustained us one day at a time and has given us signs that our siege is lifting.

I have tender affection and love for many friends who have been warriors with me in our battle. Bob Birch, Ken Blue, Paddy Ducklow, Jeff Kirby, Terry Lamb and Bob McGee have kept me afloat with their timely phone calls. I also thank the elders and staff of Grace Vineyard, who have ministered to our daily needs: Bruce and Barbara, Glenn and Kathie, Brad and Pennye, Bob and Ray, Randy and Dee.

John Abernethy, Gordon Schroeder and Randy Hylton did some valuable research which I have used. Ken Wilson intervened when my computer refused to talk to a new printer. Numerous friends and critics have read the first draft and given suggestions for improvements. Thanks to Peter Davids, Chuck Farah, Jim Hoover, Jim Hylton, Chuck Kraft, Debbie Jones, Dave Parker, Jack Taylor, Bert Waggoner, Timothy Warner, Tom White, Don Williams and John Wimber. Bill Bright kindly took the time to read the manuscript and write a foreword. This has been most helpful.

The Grace Vineyard congregation has been a pleasure to pastor from the very first day, and I love each member. My children, Faye, Scott and Meredyth, have been real troopers during all our trials and give me great satisfaction and pride. My wife, Bonnie, is the anchor of the family and the one we all love the most.

1 Introduction: Beyond Screwtape

AS FOR MANY PASTORS, THE WRITINGS OF C. S. LEWIS have always been a helpful resource to me. His apologetics aided me in student ministry, his science fiction brought me evenings of suspense, and his fairy tales brought delight to my children.

Early on I discovered *The Screwtape Letters*.[1] For years my response to the book was that it was cute and clever. I thought of myself as the well-balanced person he describes who acknowledges the reality of evil spirits without making too much of them. However, I no longer view his work as cute and clever. I now see what Lewis developed in the genre of fiction actually exists in the real world. I echo Martin Luther's perspective on this reality:

And though this world, with devils filled
Should threaten to undo us,

We will not fear, for God hath willed
His truth to triumph through us.[2]

My sensitivity to this subject was first stirred in the early 1980s. I had gone with a group of students to hand out evangelistic leaflets at a concert of Twisted Sister and Iron Maiden, two heavy-metal bands. I had given out leaflets many times before, but I had never seen anything like this. Teens (and preteens) refused my literature by saying, "I don't want it. I love Satan!" Others cursed me to my face and threatened harm to our team. Inside the concert, people bowed down as a huge smoke-spewing dragon came on stage with the musicians.

As a culture, we are now confronted at every turn by semi-occult practices and full-blown demonic manifestations. Movies honor the demonic, as in *The Exorcist*, as well as make fun of it, as in *Ghostbusters*. Action figures and television cartoons portray demons as harmless little creatures, necessary for a healthy child's imagination. Rock musicians verbalize their devotion to Satan, then propagandize for rebellion, hatred and anarchy. Bookstalls are crammed with Satanic Bibles and New Age accessories. Yuppies buy their crystals, and Shirley MacLaine headlines on "Entertainment Tonight." Local police do seminars on occult activities, and drug dealers sacrifice innocent people to gain favor with demons.[3]

This is certainly not the world of the post-war '50s, when people concerned themselves with buying their first television set to watch "Ozzie and Harriet" or listened to Perry Como on the living-room record player. No, it is a different day, and it will demand a different response by the church.

Some say this increase in evil means we are the last generation before Jesus returns. I have no settled conviction this is the case. However, it is quite evident that the battle with the enemy has become more intense.

Personally, I welcome this hour. We are no longer prevented from talking about spiritual matters because of materialistic blinders. Today, some level of mysticism is expected of everyone. It is a day much like Elijah and the prophets of Baal experienced when the challenge was issued, "Who is God?" (1 Kings 18).

As we face this challenge today, there is one major drawback. *The church is not equipped for such a battle.* We have spent our time preparing the band directors and the chaplains, but we have no trained army. But we need not despair. Once before in the history of Israel, God released the enemy in order to teach his own people to fight (Judg 3:1-4). So likewise in this hour, the church at the end of the twentieth century is learning to do spiritual warfare. We can echo King David's admission: "He trains my hands for battle; my arms can bend a bow of bronze" (Ps 18:34).

An explanation for *why* we are in a war is peppered throughout the book, but here is a brief summary. The Old Testament prophets anticipated a day when God would purge the world of evil and establish his perfect reign on earth (Amos 9:13-15; Is 65:17). In the gospels, Satan is the chief opponent to God's redemptive purposes. When Jesus announced his kingdom, it was "essentially one of conflict and conquest over the kingdom of Satan."[4] As the apostle John says, "The reason the Son of God appeared was to destroy the devil's work" (1 Jn 3:8).

Saving individual Christians is only part of a greater scheme which entails bringing all of creation out of the devil's grip and into submission to Jesus Christ (Phil 2:10-11). Jesus therefore invaded the kingdom of Satan in order to tie up the "strong man" (Mt 12:29). This binding did not mean Satan's annihilation, at least not yet, but simply the curbing of his power. He is bound, but he is on a long rope. As Oscar Cullmann has suggested, the decisive battle has been won, the tide is running in God's favor, and what remains are a few "mopping up" operations.[5] *These minor and final skirmishes are the work of the church, entering the battle zone and proclaiming release to the captives* (Lk 4:18-19). The enemy will continue to fight until he is completely obliterated (Rev 20:7-10). His tactics will vary from frontal assaults to deceptive infiltrations of the church. It is a spiritual war which will rage until all God's enemies are placed at the footstool of Jesus (Heb 10:13).

In recent years, numerous books have been written to call our attention to spiritual warfare. Michael Green's *I Believe in Satan's Downfall* and Mark Bubeck's *The Adversary* and *Overcoming the Adversary* serve us well theologically.[6] Frank Peretti's thrilling novels, *This Present Darkness* and *Piercing the Darkness,* give insight to evil spirits at work.[7] Also helpful are the numerous books on the market which expose the New Age movement and give personal testimonies proclaiming the power of Jesus Christ to set people free.

In this book on spiritual warfare, I address the subject of defeating the enemy through ordinary (and extraordinary), biblical means. Though we may commonly think of spiritual warfare as happening only in the heavenly realms, it comes in the normal course of human relationships and events—even those that are dedicated to building the kingdom of God. In some cases I describe attacks as being from evil spirits, and in others I use psychological terminology. In both cases, my assumption is that the enemy is operative in the world, stirring up conflict. Throughout this book I have used personal illustrations which come out of my pastoral ministry, changing names and surroundings to protect identity.

We will begin by surveying the nature of our spiritual warfare and the weapons we use to fight. Next, we'll consider the various war zones from which we can expect attacks. They are the world (suffering), the flesh (temptation) and the devil (demonization). We'll look at how these assaults are launched on the inner workings of the church itself, moving through the tensions which hinder church life, the conflicts with superspiritual people, and the deceptive practices of false prophets. From here we observe the way demons attack our worship, and finally, how assaults are made on Christian leaders.

> The prince of darkness grim
> We tremble not for him,
> His rage we can endure,
> For lo, his doom is sure,
> One little word shall fell him.[8]

Jesus!

I The Art of War

2 Choose Your Weapons

AS I WRITE THIS CHAPTER, I AM SITTING OUTSIDE AN OFfice building in Tijuana, Mexico. The building is clean and fashionable. The janitor of the facility has been outside for the last several hours, cleaning two eight-by-ten-foot panes of glass. At the end of his job, I notice two things: the windows are still dirty, and the job which should have taken twenty minutes lasted two hours—simply because he did not have the right tools. He had no glass cleaner, squeegee or sponge. With just a rag and a bucket of cold water, it does not matter how hard he scrubs; the grime will not go away.

The right tools always make the job easier and more effective. Similarly, in spiritual warfare, the job will not get done without the right weapons. The apostle Paul had firsthand knowledge of spiritual warfare (and its tools), and conveyed that insight to the Christians at Ephesus (Eph 6:10-20). It is to this art of warfare that this first part of the book is dedicated.

Interim Warfare

Paul begins this section of advice on spiritual warfare by saying: *"Finally, be strong in the Lord and in his mighty power"* (Eph 6:10, emphasis mine). The first word here, which is usually translated "finally" (indicating that it may be Paul's conclusion to this letter), can also be translated as "hence forward," "from now on" or "for the remaining time." With this last rendering, we can conclude that the interim between the first and second comings of Jesus will be characterized by conflict.

In this "remaining time," there will be no cessation of hostilities, no cease-fire or temporary truce.[1] As with any war, there are times of greater and lesser intensity. Soldiers do eat and sleep, but they are always aware that they are fighting in a sustained war. The devil will not take a summer vacation, a night off, or kick back for a weekend. He has one consuming passion: to destroy the glory which would come to Jesus Christ through the church. Until Jesus returns, there will be no time when the enemy is not waging war.

Preparing for War

Paul tells us to *"be strong* in the Lord and in his mighty power" (Eph 6:10, emphasis mine). To know what Paul means here about being strong, it is important to grasp the voice of the verb that he employs in this phrase.

In the English language, we are familiar with the *active* and *passive voices* of a verb. In Greek, however, there is a third or *middle voice*. It "normally expresses reflexive or reciprocal action, action viewed as affecting the subject."[2]

"Be strong" is in the middle voice in verse 10, which means one must put oneself in the environment of receiving the Lord's strength, or "become capable by means of [the Lord's] great strength."[3] But, one may ask, isn't being in the environment of the Lord's strength something which belongs to all Christians? The context of this passage suggests not. One can be a Christian, but not put oneself in a position of divine enabling.

Next, Paul tells us to "put on the *full armor* of God so that you can *take your stand* against the devil's schemes" (v. 11, emphasis mine). It is when we put on the armor of God that we enter the environment of the Lord's might. Just as the Roman soldier regarded his shield, sword and helmet as parts of his body, not optional fashion articles, so we must put on the armor of God for warfare in order to be in his strength.

"To take a stand" is a phrase which belongs to the language of war. It means to "hold a watch post" (Hab 2:1) or "to hold a critical position in a battlefield."[4]

Standing Together

Each one of us is warring for the entire body of Christ, not just for ourselves. When one flank is being attacked, then we war in that direction. If we have our armor on, then we can hold critical positions for each other. If we don't, then the enemy can penetrate the gap left by our unpreparedness.

This means we need to be aware of breaches in the wall left by those who are not able to hold their positions. If a little yeast can leaven a whole loaf, then one undefended quarter can leave our whole army open to invasion (1 Cor 5:6). This, then, is commitment to a spiritual family: supporting one another in battle. When we fail to do this for each other, people can be easily picked off by the enemy.

Over the last seven years, I have lived with the possibility that Bonnie could die of cancer. One complaint of pain or fatigue from her lips used to send me into a tailspin of despair. I was terrified she would die and leave me to live without her.

This fear was the enemy's access into my life. I was weak and vulnerable, not able to defend myself. Though I knew God had not given me a spirit of fear, I was still not able to shake it (Rom 8:15).

I was out of town at a conference when I received Bonnie's phone call telling me of her third tumor. Feeling stunned, I went back to the meeting and found the scheduled speakers had been canceled. In their place was a three-hour prayer meeting. Although they were not praying about my specific concerns, as the leaders began to pray I sensed a deep ministry going on in my soul. I knelt close to the platform and let their prayers bathe my spirit.

The next morning, as I held Bonnie in my arms, I realized the fear of her dying was gone. That's not to say I wouldn't grieve tremendously if she were to die, but the servitude to fear I had felt was completely absent. The prayers of the saints had filled in the gap, halting the enemy's work on that front in my life. This is the kind of support we all need if we are going to fight effectively.

Sharing Battle Secrets
We also stand with each other so that we might learn from each other. Because of the devil's many schemes, we need to share what we have learned about spiritual warfare.

Our enemy is tactically shrewd and ingeniously deceptive. His desire is to remain anonymous, to stay in the dark, so his ways will not be discovered. He doesn't want to be on the cover of *Time* magazine, nor to be interviewed by Barbara Walters. Rather, he does his best work covertly, picking off one person at a time. By sharing what we have learned of his methods, we expose his activities and help bring about his defeat. For this reason, one measure of spiritual maturity is how much we know about the schemes of the devil. We don't want to be always talking about the devil (which actually glorifies him), but we do want to hone each other's skill in discerning his activity.

The late British evangelist and renewal leader David Watson visited our church in the midseventies. We were an adventuresome church, but lacked spiritual power and discernment. David came to do a series of lectures in our city on renewal in the Holy Spirit.

To help prepare us for the conference, David's first talk was on spiritual warfare. Absolutely ill advised on the subject, I asked why he had chosen such a theme as his first lecture. I was eager to get into the gifts and filling of the Holy Spirit! Gently, David assured me that he knew what he was doing and that it would make sense as we went along.

He was right. As the meetings progressed, it was obvious these were not just academic lectures, but a battle for the affection of God's people. Our brief training on the subject set us in good stead for the contest we were about to undergo.

The Target of Our Warfare

Paul writes about the focus of spiritual warfare in Ephesians 6:12 (emphasis mine): "For *our struggle* is not against *flesh and blood.*" We are in a struggle with the enemy, fighting him in hand-to-hand combat. This is not in the general sense that life is a constant struggle, but in the specific sense there is an enemy who has made his presence known.

Our struggle is not against flesh and blood; it is not against people. Unfortunately, it is easy to view warfare as being against people: liberals, communists, abortionists, New Agers, humanists. Paul knows the enemy uses people and invades institutions, but he wants to get to the real source of the problem: the enemy.

"For our struggle . . . is against the *rulers,* against the *authorities,* against the *powers of this dark world* and against the *spiritual forces of evil in the heavenly realms*" (Eph 6:12, emphasis mine). The battle is against malevolent, spiritual powers which occupy the heavenlies, evil forces which rule over the world. These principalities and powers are the secret command posts which issue instructions to their earthly counterparts.[5] It is these powers, both heavenly and earthly, that we are to wrestle.

It would appear Paul was more concerned with the powers behind the personalities than he was with the personalities and institutions themselves which do evil. Here a balance must be struck. *Warring against heavenly principalities, while ignoring institutional injustices, is just as ineffective as protesting injustices without understanding the forces behind them* (Jas 5:1-6).[6]

The Bible does not give a detailed description of the heavenlies, nor does it rank demons. Thus we must be careful of any categories we might develop; any statement we make on this subject is based on speculation and deduction. Nevertheless, even Satan himself is said to be "the ruler of the kingdom of the air" (Eph 2:2).

At this point, an interesting question is raised by missiologist C. Peter Wagner and others. Can a command post be identified and destroyed by prayer, in order that more effective evangelism can take place? Wagner, in his research, has several examples of this procedure, using intercessory prayer to break powers over cities, thus allowing for successful evangelistic work.[7]

Edgardo Silvoso, commenting at the 1989 Lausanne Conference on World Evangelism in Manila, expresses support of this approach.

If there is one dominant element that has emerged in the theology and methodology of evangelism in Argentina, I would say it is spiritual warfare. It is an awareness that the struggle is not against a political or social system. Nor is it on behalf of those who are captives, but it is rather against the jail keepers, against the rulers, those in authority in the spiritual realm. The church in Argentina has learned to deal with the victimizer rather than just the victims. In so doing it has gotten to the root of the problem. The results validate this approach.[8]

This same conviction is echoed in John Dawson's helpful book, *Taking Our Cities for God.*[9] Dawson believes principalities and powers are high-ranking, supernatural personalities who seek to dominate geographical areas, cities, people groups and subcultures. He concludes, "We need to overcome the enemy *before* we employ other methods of ministry to people."[10] Dawson adds, however, that determining our city's redemptive gift is even more important than discerning the nature of evil principalities. "Principalities rule through perverting the gift of a city in the same way an individual's gift is turned to the enemy's use through sin."[11]

Destroying Enemy Strongholds

As exciting as identifying and destroying enemy strongholds may sound, a few guidelines are in order. *First, Satan is bound today in the same way he was in the New Testament: through the words and works of Jesus.* We know this because Jesus worked this way with demons, sickness, nature and death (Mk 1:21-28, 40-45; 5:35-43). There is no model in Scripture of anyone binding Satan by saying, "I bind you, Satan." Even Jesus talked of binding the strong man in a parabolic way (Mk 3:23-30). The strong man is bound, a metaphorical term indicating a curbing of Satan's power so that his house (Satan's kingdom) may be plundered. Satan's power is curbed, but he was not rendered completely powerless (Mt 16:23; Mk 8:33; Lk 22:3).[12]

Second, most of us will never deal with Satan directly, but with individual spirits or demons sent by Satan and beneath him in the kingdom of darkness. We are given only two examples of Jesus addressing Satan (Mt 4:10; Mk 8:33). Thus we have no warrant for addressing him, unless we truly run into him. Our addressing him has no place in Scripture, and surely there is no place for telling him what to do or where to go (Jude 8-10). Only the words and works of Jesus are binding on Satan. We fight principalities and powers the same way Jesus and the apostles did—by doing the works of Jesus.

Third, binding city spirits by prayer may actually be the relocation of spirits, removing them temporarily in order to minister more effectively. If, however, the open wounds which attracted demonic influence are not healed, we can expect reinfestation of the same city spirit (Mt 12:43-45). For example, if a city is governed by spirits of sexual perversion, those spirits will retake a city unless avenues of access (for example, adult bookstores, pornographic movie houses, prostitution) are closed off. Binding the ruler of the kingdom of the air must be manifested by binding institutions and healing wounds on earth.

Throughout the world today thousands of Christians are praying for citywide and national revival. "Rebuking the enemy" seems to be the most common form of intercession. However, when we analyze what has been said, we often discover Satan has been given more attention than Jesus Christ. This surely lacks proper balance. Such meetings need to focus on the lordship of Jesus Christ over a city, and include a cry of repentance by those who claim to know God, and a pleading for mercy for those still in spiritual darkness. There may be a place for binding city spirits, but too much focus on the enemy seems to play right into his attention-seeking hands.

Suiting up for War

"Therefore put on the full armor of God" (Eph 6:13). The strategy is clear, says Markus Barth: "Take up your arms, form a battle line, attack and defeat the enemy as arranged, occupy and hold the field."[13] There are seven pieces of weaponry listed to help the believer do just that (Eph 6:13-20). The model is Isaiah's God, decked out as a warrior, vindicating his people (Is 59:17). In the New Testament, God shares his armor with us so we can fight.

"Stand firm then, with the belt of truth buckled around your waist" (Eph 6:14). The belt of truth brings several images to mind. Roman soldiers used to wear leather belts to carry their swords, and to hold their tunics when they were fighting. The second image is of the priestly belt (Is 11:5).

In warfare, we must be surrounded by absolute truthfulness. The issue is not doctrinal truth, but personal truthfulness.[14] To stop the enemy, we must stop lying, whether by exaggeration or understatement, and put on integrity in all we do and say.

A lawyer taught me this important principle. He said that early in his practice he set a precedent for himself. Whenever he was questioned about the truthfulness of a statement, he would reply, "It is my habit always to tell the truth, no matter what the circumstance. And in this situation, I have abided by my principle and my practice. I have told you the truth." If this is our rule and practice, any variation will be noticeable to ourselves and others. Such truthfulness protects us from the enemy.

"With the breastplate of righteousness in place" (Eph 6:14). As Paul wrote, he was chained to a Roman soldier and probably had his armor in mind. This leather or metal corset covered the vital organs.

It is true that any righteousness we have is given to us by God, through faith (Rom 5:1). But righteousness, in the context of Ephesians 6, refers to character and conduct. Jesus was convinced the devil had nothing on him (Jn 14:30). There was no sin to exploit, no accusations to lodge. Likewise, personal righteousness, holiness and integrity, forbids the devil from having anything on us. It is our protection from exploitation.

For several years, many prophecies have been given about a coming revival in the 1990s. Even secular sociologists, like Naisbitt and Aburdene, are predicting an outbreak of religious awakening.[15] The Christian prophetic words call for righteousness on the part of any person who is to participate in this awakening. The focus will be humility rather than limelight, sacrifice rather than affluence, and glory for Jesus rather than ourselves. In all, righteousness of character is foremost.

"And with your feet fitted with the readiness that comes from the gospel of peace" (Eph 6:15). The description of prepared feet sounds somewhat like Isaiah 52:7 and the activity of evangelism: "How beautiful on the mountains are the feet of those who bring good news." But the meaning of the term "fitted" is obscure in Scripture. Most likely it means "firm footing" or "solid foundation."

I believe Paul means we are to put the gospel shoes on our feet. We are to position ourselves in the benefits of the gospel, and appropriate the promises, blessings and freedoms given to us as believers. If we do not stand in forgiveness, adoption into God's family, the power residing in us through the Holy Spirit, and our liberation from the habits of sin, then we can be easily knocked over.

Let me illustrate. The term *inner healing* is used frequently and means various things among different groups. As I understand it, inner healing is just one avenue of the sanctification process, enabling people through prayer to put on their gospel shoes. It is helping people stand in what is already theirs. For example, Sam had been saved for many years, but struggled with intimacy with God. When we counseled him, we asked if he had ever felt in his spirit the heart-cry of every believer the *"Abba, Father"* (Rom 8:15-16). Sam, however, had had no previous experience of this inner witness. As we prayed, it became apparent Sam had a long-standing conflict with his earthly father. As Sam sought God's forgiveness for the hatred he harbored against his father, the spiritual witness of his heavenly Father became a reality. Sam was fitting his feet with the gospel—accepting what was his in Christ and placing it into his life.

"Take up the shield of faith, with which you can extinguish all the flaming arrows of the evil one" (Eph 6:16). The shield Paul probably had in mind was a large, door-shaped, leather-covered shield, 2½ feet by 4½ feet. It served as protection from incendiary arrows, which were dipped in pitch and set aflame. For further protection, the shield was soaked in water to extinguish any flame on contact. The shield not only protected the individual soldier, but when many soldiers with these shields banded together and moved on the enemy like a modern tank, it posed a great military threat.

Faith is our shield. It is confidence in God's protection and guidance. In my early church experience, faith as a conscious dependence upon God was never taught. Faith was necessary for salvation, and it was proper to know how to "defend the faith," but there was never any teaching on the need for continuous faith. This was due in part to the conviction that nothing supernatural could happen after the apostles died. What I lacked in faith, I made up for in reason and effort, two highly valued virtues.

However, the New Testament expects faith from Christians. "And without faith it is *impossible* to please God, because anyone who comes to him must believe that he exists and that he rewards those who earnestly seek him" (Heb 11:6, emphasis mine). How are we to understand "pleasing God"? Do we treat it as a religious demand, or look at it more in relational terms? Probably both aspects are accurate. It is something God requires, thus it must be in our tool box. And emotionally, God responds when we exercise faith. It gives him tremendous pleasure to see us live in faith. The verse further suggests we have no ability to please God, except by faith. "Impossible" literally means "without ability." Faith is the only tool in our box which can please God.

What is faith? Faith is not so much a quality we possess, but a relationship to which we have access. We often say, "I don't have much faith today," as though faith gets used up like oil in our car. Faith in relational terms talks about intimacy with God, and facing him in an attitude of submission and worship.

Any movement of faith toward God comprises two elements. *First, we must believe that God is.* We affirm his nature as a verb and not an adjective. "He who comes to God must believe that he is." Read this way, the sentence sounds incomplete. I want to shout, "He is *what?*" But there is no qualifier. When Moses asked God what he should say God's name was, God replied, "I AM WHO I AM." Surely Moses thought, "You are *what?*" By using a present-tense verb instead of an adjective, God affirms his own dynamic presence. He is morally and spiritually active. He neither slumbers, goes to the washroom, nor takes a vacation (1 Kings 18:27). He is always actively present.

Next, we must believe God is the rewarder of those who strenuously seek him. Esau serves as grim reminder of how failure to seek God diligently when we can results in great loss and remorse later on (Heb 12:17). We must fight to trust in God's promise to reward us for seeking him, pressing back the doubt and resisting waves of self-reliance. Our efforts are duly noted in heaven.

Thus, we please the Lord Jesus when we seek his face, when we acknowledge nothing touches him like faith, when we affirm he is always dynamically present with us, and when we diligently seek him with all our heart, knowing he is our Rewarder.

A few years ago, my family and I left a very secure church situation to pioneer a new work. On May 18, 1987, God specifically told me to go to Arlington, Texas, and begin a church. To leave the financial security and friendships we had acquired over sixteen years was most difficult. The thought of striking out on our own was quite terrifying. Massive anxiety plagued me. But when impossible logistics began to loom too large, we knew we were fighting spiritual warfare. Time for the shield of faith. Not out of heroism, but out of sheer desperation, we held up our shield for God and everyone to see. After three years, with astronomical medical bills and substantial start-up costs, I am amazed at how abundantly God has provided for every need. Faith alone can protect us from the fiery darts.

Minds Clear for Battle

"Take the helmet of salvation" (Eph 6:17). The helmet was made of tough metal, either bronze or iron, with a hinged visor for protection. This image also appears in Isaiah 59:17, as Messiah, wearing his own helmet of salvation, comes to deliver those who have repented.

To put on the helmet of salvation is to accept God's protection and deliverance for our minds. Many read 2 Corinthians 10:1-6 as mystical, super-spiritual warfare against Satan. But in reality, the passage is addressing the issue of the mind as the target of the enemy. For if the enemy can gain control over our minds, he can rule. He may not stop us from being believers, but he can alter our effectiveness. We are to demolish these strongholds, patterns the enemy has programmed for us.

Our own thoughts can compose arguments and pretensions set against the knowledge of God. Therefore, these thoughts must be taken captive. This means we want to discipline conscious thoughts which produce sin, such as lust and greed. We want to discipline conscious thoughts which produce negative emotions, such as reliving an old, hurtful event. We want to take captive thoughts which reinforce wrong motives, such as telling ourselves that we really do have reason to feel personally rejected, so it's okay to avenge ourselves. We also want to capture our unconscious thoughts which lead us into sin, that lead us to dwell on negative emotions or that reinforce wrong motives. Apprehending unconscious thoughts can come through analysis, talking to someone about our emotions, or revelation, letting God reveal the hidden thoughts behind our actions.

How do we bring our minds captive to Christ? *First, we must affirm we already have the mind of Christ by the Holy Spirit (1 Cor 2:16).* Pollution from the world and temptation from our own flesh squeezes out the influence of Christ's mind. Thus, we are in need of having our minds continually renewed by the transforming work of the Spirit (Rom 12:1-2). We do not need to possess his mind, but to clear the clutter of our own minds.

Second, we ask Jesus to help us remember major thoughts, feelings and motives which have been part of our day. Jesus knows all we have thought and felt throughout the day, but it is helpful to take these thoughts, feelings and motives and place them before him. We then ask Jesus, "What is your perspective on these thoughts, feelings and motives? Give me your mind on this subject."

Our goal is to be seated with him, seeing from his perspective, rather than asking him to look from our vantage point. For thoughts which need correction, we ask for forgiveness and specific enabling to change. Other thoughts, feelings and motives need to be redeemed. They need to have the blood of Christ poured over them so we can see them as he sees them. With others, we simply ask him to take them away.

Here is an entry from my diary where I was asking Jesus to renew my mind.

Lord, today I have had some nondescript, restless feelings. What are they? I sense you are telling me I feel passed over by people. I think you are right! What is your perspective on these thoughts and feelings? I remember your warnings that these things would come. I can now also recall the specific verses you gave me in response. Without these, the enemy is confusing my mind and causing me despair. Forgive me where I have fallen prey to this pattern. Refresh my mind with your specific promises. Let my mind be yours!

"And the sword of the Spirit, which is the word of God" (Eph 6:17). The sword Paul would have been familiar with was short, 12-14 inches in length, with a pinpoint tip which could cut in any direction. In calling the sword the Word of God, Paul means that any specific statement given to us by the Holy Spirit can assist us in our defense. It may be a specific Scripture or an impression given by the Holy Spirit.[16]

At present, such a word out of Scripture is my weapon. God spoke the Scripture reference to me in a dream. When I awoke, I clearly remembered the passage, though I had no idea what it said until I read it. At first, it made little sense, but as I meditated upon it daily, it illuminated a scenario which had been plaguing me for a year. Now, whenever these haunting thoughts attack, I know it is spiritual warfare and can respond offensively with the sword the Spirit has given me.

Hearing the Lord's Battle Plan

"And pray in the Spirit on all occasions with all kinds of prayers and requests. With this in mind, be alert" (Eph 6:18). Although not usually thought of as a weapon, alert praying is a major component in spiritual warfare. To be alert means to "sleep in the open," ready for battle at any moment. It is prayer which can switch gears at a moment's notice, interceding as God leads.

We have looked at what it means to wear the armor of God, but what does it mean to "pray in the Spirit"? Praying in the Spirit is crucial to understanding and being effective in spiritual warfare, so we will look at the practice in detail here.

In Romans 8:26-27, Paul gives a very helpful explanation:

In the same way, the Spirit helps us in our weakness. We do not know what we ought to pray for, but the Spirit himself intercedes for us with groans that words cannot express. And he who searches our hearts knows the mind of the Spirit, because the Spirit intercedes for the saints in accordance with God's will.

The Spirit helps us to pray. The word "helps" means to come to the aid of someone, to take hold of the other side. This compound verb, *synantilambanomai,* is only used two times in the New Testament. In Luke 10:40, Martha cries out, "Lord, tell Mary to help me!" We can envision a heavy pot which two people needed to carry.

This is a major principle in prayer: *prayer is two-party participation.* Only when we work with the Holy Spirit do we have real prayer. Power praying is praying with the Holy Spirit rather than praying on our own. It is a false understanding of this passage to suggest that when we are not praying, the Holy Spirit is. The Luke-Skywalker, let-the-force-do-it version of prayer is false. We and the Spirit of God are both participating, taking both sides of the prayer banner and lifting it up together. As we cannot evangelize without the Spirit, love without the Spirit, or worship without the Spirit, so we cannot pray without the Spirit. As the Catholic theologian Simon Tugwell says, the first fundamental of prayer is to cry "Come Lord Jesus!"[17] We must be like Martha and let our need for help be known to the Lord.

The Spirit helps us in our weakness. Weakness is the basic New Testament word for sickness, but used in this context it takes on the meaning of helplessness, incapacity, or vagueness in praying. This is our second starting point: we realize that, alone and unaided, we are weak. People who can turn on prayer like opening a faucet may only be praying the meaningless repetitions of the pagans (Mt 6:7). Before we start to pray, it's important we take a holy, helpless pause. Catherine Marshall puts it this way:

Admittance to the school of prayer is by an entrance test with only two questions. The first one is: Are you in real need? The second is: Do you admit that you are helpless to handle that need? Why would God insist on helplessness as a prerequisite to answered prayer? One obvious reason is because our human helplessness is a bed-rock fact. God is a realist and insists that we be realists too. So long as we are

deluding ourselves that human resources can supply our heart's desires, we are believing a lie. And it is impossible for prayers to be
answered out of self-deception and untruth.[18]

This is the nature of our helplessness: we do not know how to pray as
we should. We are familiar with the subject matter, but we do not know
how to address it in prayer. How does God want us to pray in this particular situation? Each situation in life requires a unique response. There
are no absolute patterns. Therefore, we must cry out to God for a dynamic
revelation of how to pray. "Lord, I am weak. Show me how to pray."

The Spirit helps us in our vagueness by interceding for us and through
us, praying according to the will of God. In Romans 8:34, Jesus is at the
right hand of God interceding for us. In this situation, *believers are the
object of his prayer.* In verses 26-27, *believers are the vehicles of the
Spirit's prayer.* Here again is the two-party participation. The Lord Jesus,
through the Holy Spirit, shares with us his heart about a particular
matter. Then by the Holy Spirit, we pray back to the Father those desires
we believe to be from him.

To pray in the Spirit is to hitchhike on the prayer God wants prayed.
Michael Green says,

> It is a deep, free, intensive time of prayer, when the Spirit takes over
> and controls and leads the prayers. . . . It means allowing the Spirit
> of Christ to pray in us, to pour into our souls his overflowing life of
> intercession. . . . It means that he grasps the situation for us and with
> us. He frames the petitions in our lips; and he prays within us to the
> Father, with sighs too deep for words.[19]

Scripturally, there seem to be three ways in which the Spirit can lead us
to pray according to the will of God.

We can pray with words understood, or as Paul says, "to pray with [the]
mind" (1 Cor 14:15). As we are open to the Spirit of God, and not to
soulish censorship, God will flood our minds with thoughts of his nature
and presence, and with our normal speech we will begin to speak back
to him.

We can pray with words unknown, to "pray with [the] Spirit" (1 Cor 14:15), or to pray with the gift of tongues. Paul writes in verse 14: "If I pray in a tongue, my spirit prays." To pray in tongues (in the sense of 1 Corinthians 14 and not Acts 2) means that one speaks words which do not mean anything to the speaker. It is pre-conceptional speech. The speaker is not ecstatic in the strict sense of the word. He or she retains full consciousness while praying this way, avoiding any trance. The person's mind is alert and sober. The person praying in tongues has control over their speech, although they do not consciously try to produce the sounds.[20]

The Spirit can also lead us to pray without words, in groans and sighs. When Jesus healed the deaf-mute, it says he "looked up to heaven . . . with a deep sigh" (Mk 7:31-37). No words were uttered, but a burden was felt and communicated to his Father. There will be times in which we are in the same position of not uttering words, or even praying in tongues, but just groaning under the pressure of our need.

Praying in the Spirit is incredibly important during spiritual warfare. Often, as I pray for people in need, the Holy Spirit reveals the source of the battle and the particular strategy needed for the person. When I pray as the Spirit leads, there is protection and healing brought to the person.

Recently, I prayed for a man named Bert. As I prayed for him in the Spirit, I knew that he had been damaged in a previous ministry context. At that moment I did not need to hear Bert's story about that hurtful ministry time. I only needed the assurance by the Spirit that Bert's need had been revealed and, if I prayed as the Lord led, the man would come into a degree of emotional healing. And that is exactly what happened.

As we pray in the Spirit, we want to do the following things. We want to bid the Spirit to come and help: "Come, Holy Spirit!" We want to make sure our hearts are clean and we have confessed all known sin (1 Jn 1:9). We want to be saturated in the Word of God (Col 3:16) so the Scriptures flow through our prayers. We want to praise and give thanks periodically as we pray, insisting on the victory which is ours in Jesus Christ.

After we have prepared our hearts and minds in this way, we then wait and listen before we continue praying for specific needs. In this process, we dial down our own imaginations and desires for prayer. We still our hearts and listen to the Lord. Then, we are ready to pray as the Spirit leads. If we pray with others, we want to listen to them and to what the Spirit is revealing through them. And when we finish praying, we want to thank God for what he has done during the course of our praying.

Ineffective without the Right Tools

As I finish this chapter, I am still sitting outside the office building (with smudged windows) in Tijuana, Mexico. The janitor, who was so unsuccessful in cleaning the windows with only water and a rag, is now clipping the grass. I am sorry to report that he still does not have the right tools for the job. It has taken him all morning to clip a patch of grass no bigger than a golf umbrella.

It is an excellent reminder of the need for the proper, God-provided tools for spiritual warfare. This man in Tijuana has spent hours struggling along with the wrong set of equipment, and has little to show for his efforts. We, too, will be ineffective in spiritual warfare if we fight the enemy with the wrong equipment. But if we take God's weapons,

truthfulness as our belt,

righteousness as our breastplate,

the solid foundation of the gospel as our shoes,

faith as our shield,

a protected mind as our helmet,

the Word of God as our sword,

and prayer that is in the Spirit,

the Lord will equip us to defeat any enemy.

3 The Victory Is Sure

FOR MANY YEARS OUR FAMILY TOOK AN ANNUAL VACA-tion to the interior of British Columbia, Canada. Departing the city, we always drove through a long underwater tunnel to catch our main highway. I usually drove the first leg of the trip, so navigating through the tunnel was always my job.

One summer, however, I was not feeling well, so Bonnie took the wheel. As we neared the tunnel, I remembered the apprehension I usually felt as we passed through. I wondered how Bonnie would respond. Sure enough, she manifested all the symptoms I had shown. She sat bolt-upright, with both hands firmly on the wheel, commanded silence from all the children, and asked me to stay alert. When she was in the passenger's seat, she had not worried about the drive, leaving the responsibility to me. Now that she was driving, she had a new concern for our safety.

We are all in the driver's seat when it comes to spiritual warfare. We each have responsibility in this battle; everyone must be able to spot spiritual warfare, pray it back, and resist with God-given weapons. In the last chapter, we listed seven weapons useful for our battle. Now we'll talk about several more.

War in Heaven

The church at the end of the first century was undergoing devastating persecution from Jews and Gentiles alike. The Gentiles in the Roman government were jealous to have only Caesar as lord and king. To the believers living in what is now Turkey, John wrote a secret, coded message (Rev 12:1-12). The woman symbolizes Israel. From her has been birthed the Messiah and his church. The dragon is the devil, who wants to devour the people of God, but God has provided a place of protection for them.

Why was the devil so hostile toward the people of God? The conflict began with a war in heaven (vv. 7-9). Michael, the guardian angel of Israel, and all his host fought Satan and his angels. We are not told when the battle takes place, but there are various suggestions. Some see the battle as coming before creation, but this seems to be refuted by Satan's appearance before God in the Job account (Job 1:6). Others see it at the Incarnation, when Jesus contended with the devil and invaded his kingdom with righteousness (Lk 10:18). I conclude the war was fought as Jesus hung on the cross, for it was here he disarmed the powers and authorities, stripping them of their weapons and announcing their defeat (Col 2:15).

Why was Satan thrown out of heaven at this time? Because of what he had done to God's people. Five names are associated with his malicious character and person in Revelation 12:1-12.

Great red dragon (vv. 3, 9) Dragons referred metaphorically to the enemies of Israel (Ps 74:14; Is 27:1; Ezek 29:3), and his reddish color symbolizes his *murderous character* (John 8:44). For centuries, he and his unruly mob have terrorized and murdered the people of God. David Barrett, the editor of the *World Christian Encyclopedia,* estimates 40 million Christians have been martyred since the time of Christ. Only about 15,000 are known by name. About the rest, Barrett says, "Nobody wrote down their story. Their names are lost." He further concludes that each year 325,000 Christians are martyred for their faith.[1] Let everyone be apprised: our enemy is a murderous dragon.

Ancient serpent (v. 9). He is the reptile of Genesis 3 who first inspired *suspicion* about God's word. Religious cynicism in North America is the result of a plethora of deceptions sown by the enemy (Mt 13:24-28). Gone is childlike faith. It has been replaced with suspicion about God, skepticism about what he has said, and doubt about those who claim to know him.

Devil (v. 9). He is the one who slanders God and his people. He purposes to *defame and damage reputations,* not with truthful facts, but by innuendo and incomplete evidence.

Satan (v. 9). Originally, the word was not a proper name (in Numbers 22:22 RSV the angel of the Lord stands in the way as an "adversary"), but in time it became so. His name means "adversary," one who stands as our opponent in a legal contest. In this role, he was both the accuser of Job (Job 1:6-11) and the opponent of Zechariah (Zech 3:1-10).

Accuser (v. 10). Night and day Satan *accuses* people of their sin, and in Job's case he was doing it at the very throne of God. Amazingly, God's patience was held in check for this prejudicial gossip-monger (Job 1:6-12).

Since Satan no longer has access to the presence of God to make accusations (v. 8), how does he carry out his accusing? *He accuses us directly!* Every believer is susceptible to hearing damaging demonic voices. They may come through *demonic dreams,* thus the need to pray for protection before going to sleep. They may come through *words to our minds* while we are awake. Their nature is condemning, and they are easily spotted when we recognize their language. We may say to ourselves, "Where did that guilty thought come from? I have been forgiven for that sin. Oh, I know, that's the enemy's accusation. 'You evil spirit of accusation, I rebuke you in Jesus' name and command you to leave my presence.' "

Among words the enemy frequently speaks, these seem to be his favorites:

"I know you, and you're serving God with wrong motives."

"You really hate God, don't you?"

"You need to be careful, you will be left out of God's heaven."

"Boy, you're a crummy excuse for a Christian."

"Your life is really mine, and you can't change or get free."

"You can't defeat me; my demons control you!"

"You're too needy to help anyone else."

"You're stupid, and everyone thinks you're crazy."

"You will never make it, no matter how hard you try."

All are lying accusations. But, when they come, they can sound like gospel truth.

If our enemy cannot accuse us personally, *he does so through other people.* Like Peter before Jesus, their thoughts and lips become the devil's freeway (Mt 16:22-23).

Satan's Army Loses

After this war, the winners and the losers were announced. The dragon and his angels *were not strong enough* to defeat Michael and his angels (Rev 12:8). Some argue that the devil does not exist, that he is a myth of our religious culture. Others suggest that he has equal power with God, a dualism of equal but opposite powers. This group is unsure who wins the war. Yet, this verse confirms Satan as "God's devil." It is God who sets his limits, restricts his powers and banishes him when he pleases. The devil is not strong enough for God. He is not all-powerful, all-present, nor all-knowing. He is limited and confined by a superior person and power.

Given this information, it is important that we do not attribute more power to the devil than he actually has. The prominence of occult testimonies and sensational accounts of power have a tendency to leave believers fearful—or skeptical—of their opponent.[2] We do not need to fear him, nor take him lightly, but see him as a limited and defeated foe.

As a result of his banishment, Satan and his angels no longer have a *place* in heaven (v. 8). While there, Satan was constructing a foothold for his rebellion. From this strategic position, he exalted in his pride and nagged God about the sins of his people.

However, his bunker has now been blown out of heaven, giving him no place to stand. Since he has lost his *place* in heaven, he is now attempting to find a *place* on earth. So, when Paul warns us that we are to "give no *place* (topos) to the devil" by our anger (Eph 4:26-27), we know at least one *place* where he will settle if given the opportunity. *Anytime sinful habits control our lives, we provide a place for the devil, a landing pad for the demonic.* At first, they may only possess a room or two, but soon they will attempt to construct an entire house and invite all their relatives (Lk 11:24-26).

Three times we are told that *the devil and his angels were hurled down to earth* (vv. 9-10). The term for hurling down and casting out of demons has the same Greek root. *God's purpose is to fully expose the enemy. He wants them out of heaven and out of people's lives.* Such exposure will give them no place to hide, waiting only for judgment. Knowing their doom is sure, demons long to hide in the bodies of willing people. Believers can keep the door shut by continually exposing their sin to the light of Jesus' forgiveness. The enemy cannot stand where the light of God shines.

God's Army Wins

Eventually the winners are declared (12:10-11). With the death and resurrection of Jesus and the expulsion of the devil from the third heaven, God's greatest opposition was defeated. It was the D-Day of spiritual warfare. The battles from this point on are only minor mopping-up operations.

With this victory, the salvation, power, kingdom and authority of Christ became an established fact. Once and for all, the winner of the cosmic battle was declared. Since there are still minor skirmishes on earth, however, *it is incumbent upon us to manifest the presence of this victory in our own lives. We are not to get the victory over the enemy, but to act out the victory Christ has already won.*

To defeat the enemy, we must first claim the manifest presence of God: his salvation, power, kingdom and authority. How do we claim this presence? It is not by pretending pain and disease do not exist, nor is it by bargaining with God, believing only when it works. Rather, we confess the following to God and any watching evil host:

Lord, this is the word you have given to believers. It says salvation, power, kingdom and authority have been established in your name. What I see with my eyes is not all there is of the real world. Your kingdom is the real world, and you alone have power and authority here. As one little soldier, I do not have the whole picture, but I know you have won the war on my behalf. Come and manifest your victory in my life and circumstance.

Claiming Christ's manifest presence means: health and wholeness (salvation) belong to believers; assistance (power) is available in spiritual warfare; the reign of Christ (kingdom) is victorious over Satan's realm; and the right to command compliance (authority) of demons and disease has been given to the church. All four are grace weapons of the new covenant. We need not be shy in using them during this age, for in the age to come they will be of no use, since the enemy will be fully and finally subdued.

Second, the devil is defeated by the blood of the Lamb (v. 11). The enemy would encourage us to move in ways which make the blood of Christ ineffective. If we fail to confess unforgiveness, hatred or bitterness, then these areas lie outside the blood of Christ. But each sin, when confessed, is cleansed by the blood of Jesus, which defeats the work of the enemy (1 Jn 1:9). To live under the blood means to constantly appropriate Jesus' forgiveness, thereby smothering any accusation of the enemy. As Graham Powell says, demons hate to hear these confessions:

I am cleansed from all sin by the blood of Jesus (1 Jn 1:7).

I am brought near to God by the blood of Christ (Eph 2:13).

I am justified by the blood of Jesus (Rom 5:8-9).

I have redemption through the blood of Jesus (Eph 1:7).

I am sanctified through the blood of Jesus (Heb 13:12).

I have peace with God through his blood (Col 1:20).

I am in covenant relationship with God through the blood of Jesus (Mk 14:24).

I am purchased by the blood of Jesus (Acts 20:28).

The blood of Christ cleanses my conscience (Heb 9:14).

I have confidence to come into the presence of God by the blood of Jesus (Heb 10:19-22).

The blood of Jesus is precious to me (1 Pet 1:19).[3]

Third, the enemy is defeated by the word of our testimony (v. 11). As saints proclaim the effects of God's power, the enemy is pushed back in fear. Demons are aware of the finality of Jesus' victory, and each testimony is a glaring reminder of their defeat. Verbal testimonies, whether formal or informal, push the enemy back and defeat his access points.

Last, the enemy is defeated by our commitment, even unto death (v. 11). The enemy shudders when he hears we love God more than our own lives. His purpose is not to kill us, for that only transports us into the presence of Jesus. Rather, his purpose is to keep us fearing death. For those who are afraid to die, the enemy can hold anything over their heads. Our response should be, "I am not afraid of you and your threats. I am not afraid to die!"

Recently, our congregation gathered around a young missionary, recommissioning her to translation work in Southeast Asia. Independently,

God spoke to three of our leaders, saying Paulette would die a martyr's death. We did not tell her this, hoping to avoid any confusion. Two days later, she was diagnosed with lupus and subsequently had surgery. At present she is well enough to return to the field. Last week, she came to me with a dream about her own death. She explained she has known for years that martyrdom awaits her. With this opening, I was able to share our own impressions.

Whether Paulette will die soon or thirty years from now is not important. What is important is that she has faced the reality of her death and the threat made by the enemy, and she is not shrinking back. She knows she will die, but she is not stopping her work. The end of her story is yet to be written, but Paulette's courage has already been demonstrated, and the enemy has been defeated.

II War with the World, the Flesh and the Devil

4 Suffering and Persecution

SPIRITUALLY MINDED EVANGELICALS HAVE LONG WRES-
tled with the question "How can I have intimacy with God?" For
some, a season of physical sickness has been an answer. We often
hear, "I could have never grown close to the Lord without my
sickness. It was through suffering that I came to know him
more intimately."

I believe this expression is genuine, and God has become more real to
these "sufferers." In fact, I have experienced it myself. In 1983, after the
release of my book *Those Controversial Gifts* (IVP), I was bedridden for
three months and my wife went through her first bout with cancer.[1]
During this time, God drew very close to us both. It was not sin for us
to be sick, and Jesus identified with our suffering in a most special way.
So I am not unsympathetic to those who are sick, such as my wife,
especially when nothing can be done to improve the situation. However,

the theological and exegetical construct for thinking sickness is God's primary sanctifying plan for the believer is suspect at best. Did God give sickness? Is sickness the only way we can grow in intimacy with God? I believe not. Forty days of fasting would probably have the same result, without the medical expense or pain.[2]

When the notion of redemptive sickness is challenged, the accusation is usually, "You must think Christians are not meant to suffer!" But that is not so. *Christians are meant to suffer* (Acts 14:22; 1 Pet 3:17). My disagreement is over what Christians are meant to suffer and what they are not meant to suffer. I will endure anything which is mine, but I will not endure anything from the devil and call it God. In this second part of the book, we will look at war with the world, the flesh and the devil to try and sort out what we must suffer, what we must repent for and what we may rebuke in Jesus' name.

Let me contrast this view of suffering with something which happened to me a number of years ago. At the 1970 Urbana Missions Conference, I began to sense a unique work of God going on in my life. I felt an incredible burden to reach non-Christian university students on the campuses where I was an InterVarsity worker. This burden was so intense I could hardly move under its weight. Within a few months I began to make contact with people who had been touched by the "Jesus movement." This association was like pouring gasoline on an open flame. New zeal and devotion gripped my spirit. I felt the waves of revival flowing over my own soul, watering the dry corners and leaking out to others. In a matter of a few weeks, others were being renewed by this freshly found grace. Within a few months, several hundred students had come to know Christ through our evangelistic efforts.

At the same time, an avalanche of persecution fell. Four families from my home church charged me with theological heresy and brought the matter before my elders. Although my innocence was established, the ordeal produced further relational conflicts and a mistrust for my ministry. One man, who had been one of my strongest supporters, now would have nothing to do with me and forbade me having contact with students under his care. Hundreds were coming to Christ, something which had not happened before, but now it was accompanied by persecution from the ones I assumed would have supported me most.

I believe this example fits more squarely with the biblical doctrine of suffering. A proper doctrine of suffering will help us understand one component of spiritual warfare: war with the world.

The New Testament defines suffering as persecution and not as sickness. Sickness is to be treated with faith and prayer for healing. Persecution is to be welcomed, learned from, handled with endurance, and perceived as one of the enemy's chief tools in waging war against us.[3]

New Testament Suffering

The semantic field for the word *suffer* includes *needs, pain, loss, grief, defeat* and *punishment.* Since this range of meanings is so wide, we in the church have often lumped these meanings together. And since our experience in Western Christianity is usually not martyrdom or punishment, we tend to focus on pain from illness or grief from death as the main examples. However, the way we use the word in our everyday context cannot be imposed on the New Testament writers. The New Testament vocabulary of suffering is limited to external persecution by persons or demons, or to the eschatological judgment of God, and does not include human illness. A study of the vocabulary of suffering confirms this claim.

The *thlipsis* group (including *oppression, affliction, tribulation)* is used fifty-five times in the New Testament. Of those passages only John 16:21, the labor of childbirth, comes close to indicating human illness. All the other references are to persecution or oppression, or more rarely, famine or eschatological judgment.

The *paschō* word group *(suffer)* appears sixty-five times. Only in Matthew 17:15 is there any probable reference to physical illness, and in that case the illness is ascribed to a demon, a foreign spirit oppressing the individual. In fact, in Mark 5:26 the term *suffer* is applied not to the woman's illness, but to her experience at the hands of many physicians.

Even more clearly, in James 5:13-18, when a person suffers he is to pray, apparently for strength, endurance and the coming of Christ, if the previous context is our guide. But when he is ill, again a different term from suffering, he is to call for the elders and they are to pray for his healing. Thus there are two different approaches in this passage: (1) "Be patient . . . until the Lord's coming" is the response to suffering (vv. 7, 10); (2) "the prayer offered in faith will make the sick person well" is the response to illness.

James reflects the teaching of Jesus at this point. When Jesus sees illness, he never treats it as something good for the person, but rather he heals it. On the other hand, when he speaks of persecution, he treats it as something necessary in the course of history, something to be endured rather than avoided (Mk 13:9-13; Jn 15:18-27). He commands his disciples to heal the sick (Lk 10:9; Mk 6:7-13) and to endure suffering and rejection (Mt 5:10-12).

Many have assumed that Paul's "thorn in the flesh" (2 Cor 12:7) is a physical ailment. This is a classic example of reading sickness into a suffering passage. There are several reasons why Paul's thorn is probably human opposition. First, consider the context of the letter. Whether by one person or a group, Paul's apostolic authority was being attacked. They were saying he was fickle, not to be trusted, deceitful and full of corrupt motives (2 Cor 1:12-23; 3:1-3; 6:3-13; 7:2-16; 10:1-17; 11:1-33). He was suffering at the hands of his accusers.

Second, it is clear from the context of chapter eleven that human opposition plagued Paul. He describes here the litany of abuse he has suffered for the gospel: imprisonment, beatings, shipwrecks and dangers at every turn from "false brothers" (v. 26).

Third, notice the words used in 12:7 and 12:10.. The term *torment* (v. 7) refers to being struck with a fist, to be beat or cuffed about. It is used of the physical torture of Jesus in Matthew 26:67. Also, the terms used in verse 10 are synonyms for external hardship.

Last, consider the use of the term "thorn." In the Old Testament, this term refers to assaults at the hands of Israel's enemies and is no doubt Paul's meaning also (Num 33:55; Josh 23:13; Judg 2:3). Thus, I conclude Paul's thorn was not physical sickness, but rather those servants of Satan, masquerading as angels of light, who were undercutting his ministry as an apostle (2 Cor 11:14-15). As Ralph Martin says, "A chronically ill Paul does not fit well with the picture of Paul found in the New Testament."[4]

In summary, the New Testament approaches suffering and illness in two different ways. Where illness is mentioned, it is approached with prayer for healing (Jas 5:14-15). Where suffering is mentioned, it is seen as part of the spiritual warfare of the Christian, an identification with the sufferings of Christ (Rom 8:18; 2 Thess 1:5; Phil 3:10; 1 Pet 4:1), and a means of developing the Christian virtue of endurance (Rom 5:3; 12:12).

The Realm of Suffering

For years I had read, practiced and preached the popular teaching on sanctification. Suffering through sickness was honored, and suffering through persecution was shunned—except for overseas missionaries, of course. There was an attitude that there was something wrong if in the Western world one was persecuted for being a believer. I had been taught that Christians would not suffer anyway, because the rapture would occur at any moment and take away our earthly pain. Lastly, I was taught never to rock the boat.

In fact, I came to see that my early experience of evangelizing on campus was normative. Every time I heard from God and obeyed his voice, I was rocking the boat—and persecution came. *I now believe all of us are at our best when we are receiving some degree of opposition, especially when we are attempting to expand the kingdom of God.*

A friend called before I moved to Arlington. "What are you going to do in Texas?" John inquired. "I don't know for sure," I replied. "You're going to cause a whole lot of trouble, that's what you're going to do!" said my rather prophetic friend. John was right. No sooner had we arrived than the dust began to fly. There were accusations of heresy, cult involvement and authoritarian leadership. We were clearly being persecuted. Now I am not suggesting that we ought to promote trouble for trouble's sake. The trouble comes when the reviving work of Jesus begins.

Jesus spoke often of enduring persecution. A brief survey of a few passages in Matthew will highlight this point. Notice Jesus' instructions in the Sermon on the Mount (5—7); in the sending out of the Twelve (10); in the eschatological section (24); and in the Passion narratives (26-27). In other words, *kingdom expansion and spiritual warfare through persecution go hand and hand.*

The Blessings of Persecution

The presence of the kingdom, with its blessings and rewards, is assured to those who suffer. The present dynamic of the kingdom belongs to us when we are persecuted (Mt 5:10). In that moment, we access the realm where Jesus reigns. The persecution is real, not imaginary, and Jesus reigns with us in it. Whether we are the object of cutting gossip or the recipient of broken bones, the kingdom is present.

We are also called "blessed." This state of happiness is not what we feel when we are being persecuted, but what God thinks about us as we endure it.[5] Expositor William Hendriksen puts it this way: "Already heaven's favor is resting upon them."[6]

The same moment evil lips speak against us falsely, God utters a blessing on our behalf. God not only utters an earthly blessing when we are persecuted, he also reserves for us a future heavenly reward (v. 10). Such assurances, however, do not ease the pain of feeling forsaken by God (Mt 27:46). The Father knows everything happening to us, and we are valuable in his sight (Mt 10:29-31). Persecution cannot undo the Father's will for us, nor will it affect his care for us.

My friend Jeff had an acute experience of this kind of persecution. He called to tell me that he had been voted out as pastor of his church. "George, I didn't do anything wrong!" It was true. At the time, it was little consolation to him when I told him he was blessed for his struggle. Though we may feel abandoned at the time of our persecution, from God we have a "Well done!"

Influence that Brings Persecution

Persecution is a sign we are having prophetic influence. To be persecuted is to join the company of the Old Testament prophets (Mt 5:12). Anyone who is aggressive for the kingdom of God is going to appear prophetic to anyone who is committed to personal peace and prosperity. Therefore, we should expect retaliation when we press the edge. This opposition is really a compliment, for people now take us seriously enough to see us eliminated. The world is not interested in persecuting ineffective and unfruitful people; only those who shake things up are hassled.

One who suffered persecution because of his influence was Charles Simeon (1758-1836), the trainer of Anglican preachers. He was aggressively opposed when he assumed his pulpit at Holy Trinity Church, Oxford, England. Wealthy pew holders refused to listen to him preach. Not only that, but they locked up their boxes so no one else could use them either. He was spat upon, dashed with eggs, and harassed constantly in his first decade of preaching. Why? He was prophetic to a people who only wanted religion.[7]

I also think of several friends who have been recently fired from a prominent seminary. Their theological views had not strayed in any major way, nor was there any concern about improper moral conduct. Rather, the central focus lay in their prophetic stance regarding the work of God and the spread of his kingdom.[8] Many were sorry for these brothers, but I had another reaction. It dawned on me that getting fired might have been God's way of saying, "Your ministry is the most prophetic it has ever been. They persecuted the prophets, now they are persecuting you."

If Jesus was gifted and not revered, then we can expect not to be respected either (Mt 10:24-25). I have seen this clearly in the last few years. Previously, arguments against the cessation of spiritual gifts were based upon Scripture, theology and history. Popular argument has now shifted to suggest that the devil inspires healings, tongues, prophecies and other gifts. Certainly there are cases when cults and other groups pervert these gifts. But the charge that Bible-believing, morally upright, doctrinally orthodox Christians, praying in Jesus' name, are empowered by the devil to exhibit these gifts is incredible. Thus, this passage is being fulfilled once again: Christians who practice the gifts of the Spirit, modeled by Jesus, are being persecuted for this type of prophetic influence.

Being prophetic also means we will be passed over (Mt 27:21-22). Jesus was passed over for Barabbas, and we too will be passed over. If we stand for righteousness, we can expect not to be included where other values reign. Kevin was a salesman with a six-figure income. As a believer, his conscience was being tutored by the Holy Spirit and Scripture. He knew his company was not acting in a moral manner, so he blew the whistle. Instead of confronting the issues and making the hard decisions for change, Kevin's supposedly Christian company found it easier to let him go. He did not play the game, so he lost the part.

Being prophetic will also gain us mixed responses from those who do not like us (Mt 11:16-19). One minute they want us to dance, the next minute they want us to mourn. One minute they want change, the next minute change is too fast. It is good when God works. But it's bad when he disrupts agendas.

I experienced this kind of reaction when I was invited to speak at a denominational conference. I asked for freedom to speak whatever God was revealing to me out of the Scriptures, and was assured this was permissible. My first lectures were received coolly.

Several days later, the Spirit began to penetrate the hearts of some of the younger leaders, and a minor revolt began to take place. They wanted their churches to be renewed and were prepared to pay the price. Not everyone there appreciated the Spirit's work, however.

A few months later, I received an official letter of appreciation for speaking. However, most of the first page was taken up with objections to a few things I said. The last paragraph, almost in the form of a post-script, mentioned a prophetic word which had been spoken to the group. The word was that seven pastors, present in the meeting, were involved in adultery, and if they did not repent, God would remove them from the ministry. The writer of the letter concluded with this comment: "The last pastor just came and repented!" Now I hope the irony in this will be evident. They did not like my dress, my lecture style, or my word selection, but seven of their pastors were "smoked out" for adultery. At once they were hostile to ministry and thrilled that sin was revealed. Kingdom work does not play to the crowd, and thus we cannot look to the approval of others to set our agenda.

Of course, we are occasionally persecuted because we are prophetic at the wrong time, to the wrong people (Mt 7:6). Occasionally, when sharing on the renewing work of the Spirit, I have realized it was the wrong thing to do. I had become a promoter of the Holy Spirit, rather than a co-laborer with the Spirit. The Spirit was telling me not to speak any longer because the ground was unfruitful. There was no hearing ear, no hungry heart, and to continue was useless.

One misconception about operating prophetically is that we will always know what to say; but this is not the case. However, we are given assurances that the Lord will give us words (10:19-20). I was once coerced into publicly debating two university professors on the merits of Christianity. My partner informed me, halfway through the debate, that his wife was expecting him for dinner, and he promptly excused himself. I was left to take on two fire-breathing, apostate, former clerics.

In many ways I was out-classed, but I continued to pray God would give me a word which would swing the tide. Strangely, the Spirit prompted me with a quote from the Jewish philosopher Barnard Buruch: "Every man has the right to his own opinion, but no man has the right to be wrong in his facts." When I uttered these words in the closing moments of the debate, the audience suddenly shifted and began to applaud wildly. Buruch's words have no power in themselves, but I knew God had given me words to handle this particular situation.

It should not shock us to realize that Jesus' main opposition came from religious leaders (Mt 23). Is it any different today? Have the scribes and Pharisees passed away with the apostles? Unfortunately, their spirit is still active. It is for this community that Jesus reserved his harshest comments. My friend Ken Blue has observed, "If we endure the persecution of the church, we might get the chance to be persecuted by the world."

Spiritual awakening also causes division within families (Mt 10:21, 34-36). Early Christians were accused of breaking up families, a claim also leveled against missionaries today. I remember three young men who were rejected by their parents when they joined our church. They were no longer allowed to go into their parents' home or even have a meal with them. Visitation was limited to a few minutes on the porch, two or three times a year. Their own parents had become their enemies.

Endurance

In spite of persecution, we must endure to the end (Mt 10:22). The New Testament word for *standing firm or endurance* is comparable to flexible steel, able to bend without breaking. In the midst of the hatred, the persecuted believer will feel the blows of resistance just as painfully as any other human being. Rejection for the Christian feels the same as it does for a non-Christian. The difference lies in the way we receive it. Aided by divine assistance and the certainty of a coming judgment day, the believer bends, but does not break. Under each assault there will always be the temptation to quit. But giving up is the signal that we have thrown in the towel and removed ourselves from the battle. We mustn't contemplate admitting defeat if we want to remain in the fight.

A modern substitute for endurance is drugging ourselves so we feel no pain (Mt 27:33-34). But Jesus did not anesthetize his rejection and pain by dulling his mind with drugs. So there is no room for us to chemically dull the torture people would heap upon us.

Sometimes the persecution is so intense we must flee in order to endure (Mt 10:14, 23). There is evidence that Christians fled Jerusalem to Pella in the Transjordan between 66-67 A.D. Eusebius indicates the action was in response to a prophetic word before the Roman general Titus took the city.[9] This word has contemporary examples in the migrations of pacifist groups from Russia and other parts of Europe.

Responding to Persecution

Our response to persecution is not to passively grin and bear it, but rather we need to go the second mile and manifest active love (Mt 5:38-48). Jesus' words deny us the opportunity of seeking revenge. Our only alternative is to love and pray for our enemies. With such love, we give up the right to make any pronouncement on the spirits and characters of those who hurt us (Mt 7:1).

The temptation to judge another may mean that God is pointing out a log in our own eye (Mt 7:3-5). We may be innocently persecuted, and at the same time God may choose to refine our character by pointing out our own shortcoming.

Hebrews 12 speaks of the discipline of the Lord. The context of the chapter, as well as the meaning of the word discipline, suggests that refinement comes by way of opposition from other people. Jesus endured it (Heb 12:3). Jesus faced the hassle of getting up every day, knowing he would encounter opposition from people. Although he did not have any sin to be purged, he still had things to learn from the opposition he would suffer (Heb 2:14-18; 4:14-16; 5:8).

We, too, have much to learn from the opposition we face as we advance the kingdom of God. This persecution, which goes on all the time for all of us, can eat away at our strength and cause us to want to give up. But it is just spiritual warfare, and it is common to all those who push against the enemy's camp. If we are pressing for the kingdom, we have probably experienced situations similar to those described in this chapter. Hopefully, we now have a better idea of what is going on and can respond more biblically. It's not circumstances we are fighting, it's war.

5 Trials and Temptations

AN OUTBREAK OF SEXUAL IMMORALITY AMONG CLERGY led reporters to interview psychologists and seminary professors about its cause. One professor was asked what his school was doing to prevent the problem, since one of their former students had been criminally charged. The professor replied, "We had two chapels on the subject this year." This is a tragic comment. Two chapels cannot stamp out sexual immorality any more than two fire extinguishers can put out a forest fire. It's too little, too late. There are many things which could be done to prepare pastors for this problem. One would be learning to manage temptation.

Temptation
Temptation is the most elementary level of spiritual warfare. It is perhaps

the obvious form of war with the flesh. The Greek word for temptation *(peirasmos)* is morally neutral and can be translated as temptation, testing or trials. There is nothing inherent in the word to make it good or bad. The context alone determines its definition. "I tempted my child with courage" is different from "I tempted my child with rebellion." To discern more about temptation we must ask three questions: Who is inspiring the temptation? What is the purpose of the temptation? Then, how do we respond to the temptation?

Temptation can come from a variety of sources. *First, it can be inspired of the devil, with the purpose of leading us to sin.* God is never the author of temptation (Jas 1:13), but as with Jesus, he may permit the devil to engage us for a season (Lk 4:1-2). With such assaults, we have the choice to cooperate or not.

Second, temptation can be inspired from our own flesh (Jas 1:13-15). It arises because of the desires of the flesh. Here, too, we have the choice to cooperate or not.

Third, although God never tempts, he does allow trials for our growth and maturity. As with temptation, we have a choice to cooperate or not. If we choose not to work with God, the trial becomes an avenue of temptation for the devil and our own flesh. God-given trials, when properly received, are opportunities for us to grow in the Lord.

Our primary concern in the midst of a temptation or trial should not be "Where is this coming from?" but "How can I handle this situation in a godly manner?" This is the most productive question to ask.

For several years, I followed the story of the Seventh-Day Adventist pastor in Australia who lost his baby daughter in an attack by a dingo dog. Meryl Streep stars as the pastor's wife in the movie re-creation *A Cry in the Dark.* Through a strange set of circumstances, the pastor's wife was charged and jailed for the murder of their child. Three years later, subsequent evidence cleared her of the charges, and she was released. During the entire ordeal the pastor was struggling to answer the *why?* of his trial. The media wanted to know why. His church wanted to know why. And the pastor himself wanted to know why. But the reason for the trial was not resolved for Job, and most likely it will not be for us. Our only recourse is to say, "God, you have permitted this circumstance in my life. Someday you may tell me why and where it is coming from. Until then, I wish to respond in a way which is truly human, and at the same time bring glory to you. Strengthen me to respond every hour and every day according to your character."

When Paul says, "no temptation has seized you except what is common to man" (1 Cor 10:13), he is referring to the three avenues we have mentioned: the devil, our own flesh and trials from God. Each of these avenues is common to every man; even Jesus endured two of them (Heb 2:18). Temptation can give some of us great difficulty, while others may handle it quite well. The difference lies in how we respond when it comes; it's harder for us to combat when we give into its demands.

Resisting temptation is a process. No matter where we are on the scale of resistance, if we cooperate with God, he will be faithful and not allow us to be pushed over the brink. He will provide us a way of escape, so we can get through the temptation—either to endure it or get out of it. This is a promise to claim in the midst of spiritual warfare. We need to memorize it, pray it and preach it to ourselves daily. It is an unalterable promise from God and will not be shaken by our circumstances. He knows the frailty of our frames and what we can endure. The heavenly grandstands are full of the faithful dead (Heb 12:1) cheering us on to the finish line. They are saying, "Don't give up! We have done it and so can you!"

Escaping Satan's Temptation
Scripture suggests at least five ways of escaping temptation from the devil.

Prayer. We can pray *prevention prayers,* prayers which keep us from entering Satan's arena. "And lead us not into temptation, but deliver us from the evil one" (Mt 6:13). This prayer acknowledges our weakness and God's greatness. We do not want to meet the enemy; therefore, we call upon God to keep him distant. It is a beseeching which pleads, "God, keep me from unnecessary and harmful temptations. Rescue me from the threat of the evil one." As James Houston points out, this prayer is also useful for our own heart.

So we cry out to the father: lead me through all the evil tendencies of my heart. Help me to overcome the temptations of my temperament. Change inside me the evil tendencies of my own personality as it relates to other people. Protect me from the temptations of my own age group in the phases of life: passionate when young, cynical when middle-aged, self-pitying when old and lonely. Save me from the temptations of our culture, the modern world in which we live. For in all these realms, and above all to my sinful heart, I am seducible.[1]

This petition is from the Lord's Prayer and is befitting for our daily use. Like a grace covering, it is to be put on as clothing every day. As the Augustinian canon Walter Hilton taught some 600 years ago, the Lord's Prayer is a well-balanced theological discipline and should precede any free form of prayer.[2] The Lord's Prayer is most needed when we know we are about to confront a difficult problem.

I have counseled people who knew in their spirits when some disaster was about to come to their family. Yet they felt paralyzed to do anything about it. I instructed them to pray this daily, covering every family member, their jobs and possessions. Such prayers have then cooperated with God's hand, holding off the incoming assault.

Next, we can pray *prayers of protection.* "Watch and pray so that you will not fall into temptation. The spirit is willing, but the body is weak" (Mt 26:41). Sieges of temptation may need extended seasons of prayer to be kept at bay. We need to pray, "God, protect me from this assault. Keep my mind focused upon you and your work. Empower me to be diligent in prayer and to overcome this temptation." Many godly people endure protracted temptations by increasing their time in prayer and fasting. The idle mind is the devil's workshop; thus it is necessary to occupy the mind with prayers in the Spirit. We cannot resist the enemy with mere bodily strength. We must fight with our spirits. We must discipline our bodies by the rod of the Spirit, for when the body rules, sin is near. But when our spirits lead, God is near.

We can also pray *rebuking prayers.* "But even the archangel Michael, when he was disputing with the devil about the body of Moses, did not dare to bring a slanderous accusation against him, but said, 'The Lord rebuke you!' " (Jude 9). Michael was careful not to dialog with the devil, to argue or reason with him. He did not stand on his own authority, but cried out, "The Lord rebuke you!"

Likewise, we can say to the enemy: "The Lord charge *you* with interfering with his work. The Lord charge *you* with this temptation. This did not come out of my flesh, nor from God. This temptation is *charged to your account.*" Such a prayer is especially useful when we have been suddenly tempted by the enemy. Reeling from the moment, we may wonder, "Where did that come from?" Occasionally, when ministering to people in prayer, the enemy has planted in my mind horrible thoughts about the person I'm praying for. There was no logical reason for these thoughts. They were simply missiles of temptation, sent to confuse and disrupt. At those moments, we need to aggressively lay the temptation back at the feet of the one who inspired it.

Another way of rebuking the enemy is to demand he be silent. Jesus used this prayer when he confronted the demonized man and commanded the evil spirits to "be quiet" (Lk 4:35). The image is of muzzling an animal so it cannot open its mouth. In the protection and authority of Jesus' name, we too can command the enemy to cease his chatter. This is most necessary when he is attacking our minds with polluting and confusing thoughts.

Last, we can pray *prayers of dismissal.* "Jesus said to him, 'Away from me, Satan!' " (Mt 4:10). This prayer addresses the one who is provoking the temptation. Although we may never have occasion to use this prayer against the person of Satan, we will use it often when harassed by spirits. "You spirit of confusion, I demand you leave in the name of Jesus." We address the enemy as specifically as possible, naming his character and the area of attack. Such an address uncovers his hiding place and releases a direct arrow of light, causing him to flee.

Nightly prayers are a ritual in our home, and it's usually the children who make the request: "Mom, come and pray with me!" When one of our children was quite young, she uttered this prayer: "Lord, I'm too tired to pray tonight, so I want you to know my prayer is the same as last night, *only with sincerity.*" Everyone gets tired of praying, and it is easy to have a ditto prayer like Faye's. Yet warfare praying must be aggressive if it is to be useful. It cannot be prayed in a stupor or as an afterthought. Prayers of deliverance, protection, rebuking and dismissal demand an alert spirit and an aggressive posture.

Fleeing. This is the second way we are to escape temptation from the devil. We are not to argue or reason with demonic temptation, nor are we to wrestle with it to see how strong we are. We are to run! (See 1 Cor 6:18; 10:14; 1 Tim 6:11; 2 Tim 2:22.)

Many secular sources now advocate the same method in response to drugs, alcohol and "unsafe" sex. We are exhorted: "Just say no!" Even small children are taught to deter sexual abuse by shouting "No!" and leaving the room as quickly as possible. It shows a lack of Christian maturity to sit and endure when we see a set-up coming. No explanation is necessary; just say *no,* and leave.

Using Scripture. A third response to temptation is to quote Scripture. Jesus used the Word of God as his reply to the devil's traps. He did not attempt to explain the Word, to defend its reasonableness, nor the reliability of its source. He simply stated what God said, and let it stand as his sufficient and final argument. (See Mt 4:1-11; Lk 4:1-12.)

Our enemy is not a worthy opponent with whom to debate. We will not win any arguments with him, because God's truth is something he avoids. Besides, he is a liar by nature. We will meet him in situations with other people. When this happens, we are tempted to try to persuade them to our side. We can save our breath; the fewer words the better. End such no-win situations as quickly as possible by saying something like: "I cannot do what you are saying. I take my counsel from God's Word, and he will not let me do this. Good day!"

At other times, we may need to quote exact Scripture references which speak to our situation. For example: "I am sorry, but the Bible says, 'What would it profit a man to gain the whole world and to lose his own soul?' What you are suggesting would cause me to lose my life."

It is not only toward people that such responses are required, but also in lonely moments when our own flesh is tempted or an evil spirit assaults us. Our rebuking and dismissal prayers will be greatly enhanced by God's Word. "I rebuke you, spirit of anxiety. My God will meet all my needs according to his glorious riches in Christ Jesus. Be quiet and leave me now!" (Phil 4:19).

Resistance. The fourth method of resisting temptations of the enemy is resistance. "Submit yourselves, then, to God. Resist the devil, and he will flee from you" (Jas 4:7). The enemy turns and leaves when we firmly take our stand, verbally and volitionally. We let him know in no uncertain terms that we have staked our position with God and have no plans to move.

"Mercy, mercy" is a game of wrist wrestling which many children play. The game ends when one child is made to cry "Mercy!" Physical strength is necessary to win, but equally important is the determination not to lose. It will keep one in the game for a long time. Likewise with us, resisting the devil requires mental toughness which refuses to give in to temptation. We make the choice to resolutely stand for righteousness as we tell the enemy to back off.

Divine Assistance. The fifth way to fight temptation is provided straight from heaven. Jesus has promised to help us when we call on his name, and he intercedes on our behalf.

"Simon, Simon, Satan has asked to sift you as wheat. But I have prayed for you, Simon, that your faith may not fail. And when you have turned back, strengthen your brothers" (Lk 22:31-32). The devil, with God's permission, wanted to cut loose on all the disciples (the first *you* is plural), and especially on Peter. But Jesus prayed for them to endure.

Likewise, when the devil cuts loose on us, Jesus is praying that our faith will not fail (Rom 8:34). It should give us great confidence to realize Jesus has never prayed a prayer that God the Father did not answer. This leads me to ask: "Jesus, pray for me. Talk to the Father about me. Pray for my protection."

Not only does Jesus know how to pray for us, he knows how to get us out of seemingly inescapable situations. "The Lord knows how to rescue godly men from trials and to hold the unrighteous for the day of judgment" (2 Pet 2:9).

Although Jan was a Christian and had been raised in a good church, she had become involved in a Satanic cult. There, she was the object of sexual abuse and even participated in ritual murder. Jan knew she was doomed to die, and cried out to God for help.

One evening she was picked up by a carload of cult followers who told her that something special would happen to her that evening. She knew it meant her death. As they drove along, Jan prayed to Jesus for a way of escape. "We pulled up to a stop light in the middle of the city," she said. "I prayed to God and then said, 'Excuse me, I want to get out.' " Strangely blinded and docile, the Satanists let her out of the car and into freedom.

Jan's story is an example of loving, divine assistance. Eleventh-hour escapes are not something we take for granted. But when we have done all we can, it is of great comfort to realize that Jesus is praying for us and is able to deliver us from hostile situations.

Temptation from the Flesh

The second avenue of temptation is from our own flesh. It is dishonest to blame the devil for sin when the problem lies in our own hearts (Jas 1:14-15). Self-discipline is often promoted as the major antidote to fleshly temptation. This attribute is surely necessary, but the first line of defense against our flesh lies in the cross (1 Cor 9:24-27; Gal 5:22-23). It is the work of Christ which first and foremost subdues our flesh. The gospel is not only our means of securing eternity, but it is also our means of deliverance on earth.

What is our response to the following statement? "Since we are born again by the Spirit, we need no longer sin." Now, I am not saying we can ever attain sinless perfection. Believers do sin, but because of Christ's life in us, we are no longer slaves to sinful patterns. Such liberation is our grounds for fighting temptation. Paul develops this principle in Romans 5—8, using four key verbs: *knowing, reckoning, presenting* and *walking.*

Knowing. Our starting place for fighting temptation is to know the truth. In Romans, Paul inquires, "Don't you *know* that all of us who were baptized into Christ Jesus were baptized into his death?" (Rom 6:3, emphasis mine). Ignorance of our life in Christ will always leave us defeated. He proceeds to fill in the gap by saying: "For we *know* that our old self was crucified with him so that the body of sin might be done away with, that we should no longer be slaves to sin" (Rom 6:6, emphasis mine). Without knowing what Paul tells us, we cannot survive temptation.

What do we see when we visualize the cross of Calvary? Do we see only the crown of thorns, the blood from Jesus' side, or his nail-scarred hands? If this is all we see, then we are perceiving only half the picture. We should also see ourselves hanging there with Jesus, for if we have identified with Christ through faith, then we have been crucified with Christ (Gal 2:20).

Some talk about the crucified life as though it were something we did everyday: get out of bed, have breakfast, dress and climb upon our cross. There is a place for denying ourselves daily, but it is also the case that the moment we trusted in Christ, we died once and for all (Lk 9:23).

Since we are obviously alive, we might wonder what part of us is supposedly dead. Our "old self," our former manner of life, the person we once were is dead. So I can say that on November 5, 1964, George Mallone was killed. The immoral, drunk, cheating, lying, insecure and judgmental

George was put to death. The penalty for that former manner of life was executed upon me as I identified with Christ on the cross.

If crucifixion is not final enough, notice that we have also been drowned and buried (Rom 6:3-4). To be immersed in the waters of baptism is a picture of our death. The person we once were has been drowned. The metaphor then switches to a grave plot where dirt is thrown upon us. If these pictures are true, we cannot possibly blame our sinful habits upon a residue of our former life, since it is dead. We are not justified in saying, "When I was a non-Christian I lived with all kinds of sins. When I became a Christian, these things fell off for a while, but now they have crept back into my life." No, the "old self" is dead. The former life has been crucified, drowned and buried. It cannot be blamed for our sinful habits.

If we cannot blame our "old self" for these sins, where do they come from? They come from *our willingness to cooperate with indwelling sin still left in us.* Notice what God has purposed in the death of the person we once were. His purpose is that the "body of sin" might be made powerless, so we would no longer obey its sinful impulses and be its slave (Rom 6:6).

In our lives, there is the capacity for sin and rebellion against God. As non-Christians, this tendency overpowered us so we could do nothing without its permission. When we came to know Christ, that capacity was not annihilated. We still can sin. But that capacity for sin was paralysed; it no longer has the power to enslave us. We do not have to live with patterns of sin any longer. The only way this impotent force can manifest itself again is *when we want it, excuse it* or *nurture it.*

Reckoning. In the normal Christian life, believers will find themselves tempted to participate again in sinful patterns. When we see such patterns beginning to develop, we need to take stock of and affirm who we are in Christ (Rom 6:11). This is the reckoning Paul speaks of, and the verb tense he uses indicates that it is to be an ongoing process: "Count yourselves dead to sin."

We acknowledge that our behavior is sinful and displeasing to God. We acknowledge that this behavior from our former life does not still have power over us, since that life is dead and we are new creatures. We then confess that this behavior is coming from the residue of sin still within us. Finally, we acknowledge we have been raised with Christ and live in new life with him (Rom 6:4).

The familiar complaint from those who feel mastered by their sin is this: "I just can't stop sinning, no matter how hard I try!" If I believed this, I would have to surrender the gospel.

My response is to probe: Is the person truly born again? Does he understand what Jesus has done for him on the cross? Does she want to leave her sin?

I want to know about the reality of their Christian experience. Modeling after Acts 2:38, I ask if they have *repented* and turned around from their sins. What did they put away when they came to Christ? Next, did they *believe* in the Lord Jesus Christ? Do they understand the significance of his name as Lord, Jesus and Christ? Did they *receive the gift of the Holy Spirit* when they believed? Do they have the inner witness of the Spirit's cry of *"Abba,* Father"? Do they know they belong to God (Rom 8:15)? And were they *baptized* in water? If any step along the way has been missed, I go through it with them until it is firmly believed and received. My purpose in this is to correct any "bad birthing," which always produces weak Christians.[3]

Next, I examine their knowledge of Christ's death and its impact on their life. We review the principles of Romans 6:1-14, explaining step-by-step what has transpired. I assure them that they do not have to sin— not because of self-discipline, but because of the life of Christ that now resides in them.

I then lead them through the reckoning process, establishing a spiritual reality check for their lives. It is helpful here to examine their motivations for sinning. Why do they do what they do? Uncovering the motive will give us an opportunity to minister to the hurts which often produce sin. For example, attention-gathering behavior may have its roots in a negligent parent who refused to express affirmation. Healing of that memory or relationship, paired with knowing and reckoning, may be what it takes to see their pattern of sin halted.

Presenting. The third action Paul encourages us to take in our fight against temptation is to *present* or *offer ourselves* to God (Rom 6:13, 19). This present-tense command can also be translated as *to yield,* to put ourselves at someone else's disposal.

My oldest daughter, Faye, taught me a little about this principle. Faye took piano lessons for several years. Practices were never very successful if she was sent off to do them by herself. But if her mother was sitting next to her, modeling the technique and coaching in the reading, her practice times were very fruitful. Faye was putting herself at Bonnie's disposal, placing herself in her hands.

Likewise, if we put ourselves at Jesus' disposal, *he supernaturally begins to produce his life in us.* Jesus resides in his believers, modeling for us and coaching us. Notice it is our bodies we are to put at his disposal (6:13). God is not concerned with the dedication of religious feelings; he wants our bodies—eyes, hands, feet, mouths, minds and genitals. The tense of the verb suggests that we are to do it right now, without delay, and once for all. "Lord, these are your hands. What do you want them to do? These are your eyes. What do you want them to see? This is your mouth. What do you wish me to say? These are your feet. Where do you wish me to go?"

Walking. The last key verb for contending with temptation from the flesh is *walking,* living according to the Spirit (Rom 8:4). Paul contrasts this to living by means of the flesh. To live this way, we must have minds controlled by the Spirit, not by the flesh (Rom 8:6, 9).

But we also need the equipment of the Spirit, the power and the resources of the Spirit, to "put to death the misdeeds of the body" (Rom 8:13). God has redeemed us and is in the process of changing our character (2 Cor 3:18; Rom 8:29). By the Holy Spirit, because of the redemption available in Jesus, we are led in the process of killing off evil activities and thoughts.

John Stott describes the mortification process this way:

Mortification . . . means a ruthless rejection of all practices that we know to be wrong; a daily repentance, turning from all known sins of habit, practice, association or thought; a plucking out of the eye, a cutting off of the hand or foot, if temptation comes to us through what we see or do or where we go. The only attitude to adopt towards the flesh is to kill it.[4]

This is not an exhortation to more self-effort, but a legitimate expectation given our crucifixion with Christ and the power boost we can expect from the Holy Spirit.

Knowing what Christ has done for us on the cross is our means of fighting temptation. We count ourselves as dead to the trap of sin and alive to doing the will of God. We therefore dedicate our bodies to God, using them according to his will. In the process, we yield to the assistance of the Holy Spirit to subdue any sinful habits which might come our way.

Trials from God

In God's economy, trials are allowed in our lives, and are to be viewed as distinct from temptations. In James 1:1-16, we are given a theology and practice for trials and temptations. We are told their sources and the appropriate response to each.

Trials are untimely outward afflictions which we fall into (Jas 1:2). The traveler on the Jericho road, who became the recipient of the Samaritan's care, did not plan to be mugged; he fell into it (Lk 10:30). Trials are divine accidents, which happen by God's permission. By contrast, *temptations are inward incitements, solicitations from our own desires or stirrings from the enemy.*

Trials are meant for our good (Jas 1:2-4). They are productive events in the life of the Christian. Although they may be unpleasant, they do have redeeming value. Even though trials come with good intent, a wrong response can lead us into sin. To take this wrong option is to deny the reason for the trial and leave us bitter toward God. However, *temptations come at us with a sinister motive,* having no concern for our well-being (Jas 1:14-15). Temptation's only purpose is destruction.

Trials produce maturity in the Christian (Jas 1:4). The goal of the Christian walk is to be complete and mature, and there can be no perfection without trials, as surely as there can be no crowns without the cross (Mt 5:48; Col 1:28). *Temptations are designed to lure us into sin and death; they are the bait for our entrapment* (Jas 1:15).

Trials come to us from the loving hand of God (Jas 1:16-18). They do not escape his attention, nor frustrate his plans. *Temptations flow from the devil and our own desires* (Jas 1:14).

Trials are to be welcomed (Jas 1:2). We are not to resent them as inconvenient intruders, but receive them as friends. At that moment we are to be supremely happy—a step of faith, for sure—embracing all the godly fruit the trial is producing in our lives. We are not to squirm out of it, but let the trial run its full course. In such moments, we will need incredible wisdom, which God promises to give us if we ask in faith (Jas 1:5). As we have said, *temptations are to be confronted by prayer, fleeing, Scripture and resistance.*

Discerning between Temptation and Trial

As we have found, our response to temptations and trials is critical. But there can be confusion about the source. Is it from God? the devil? Is it from the devil, at the permission of God? Or from God, with interference by the devil? The following guidelines will help us discern between temptation and trial.

If a temptation to sin seems unusual to our normal pattern, or we are overwhelmed to do something evil which we have never considered before, and if it hits from the blind side—this is temptation from the devil.

If the temptation does not leave with prayer, fleeing, Scripture and resistance, then it is most likely a temptation of our own flesh. It is then to be countered with the benefits of the cross: knowing, reckoning, presenting and walking.

If we have taken steps to contend with the devil and mortify our own flesh, and the problem continues, then we may need deliverance from demons and/or inner healing.

Even if we have gone through all of these steps, we can anticipate a counterattack from the enemy. Each time we resist him, it will be easier to identify the temptation and dispense with it. There is no one-time fix for temptation. But it *can* be beaten.

Last, a word about trials from God. Every afternoon my children return from school with several pages of homework. They are assigned problems to solve in order to successfully understand the material. God also has problem assignments for his children. These are clearly from his hand and will lead us into maturity as we tackle them one day at a time.

6 Twentieth-Century Ghostbusters

THEOLOGICALLY, I HAVE BELIEVED IN DEMONS SINCE MY conversion. Dr. Merrill F. Unger, the author of *Biblical Demonology,* was in my home church, so academically the subject was credible.[1] Personally, however, I had no encounters with demons until 1984. Up until then, I had felt sure that such activities were confined to occult practices and foreign cultures. But since 1984 I have witnessed numerous cases of demonization.

Running into Demons

I had a very memorable occasion of running into demons in the winter of 1985. Along with another pastor, I was speaking at a church conference. Our theme for the weekend was from Matthew 4:17: "Repent, for the kingdom of heaven is near."

The first two meetings seemed to have little effect, and we were getting discouraged. On Saturday afternoon, we arranged to have lunch with John White, the author and psychiatrist. Looking for help, we invited John and his wife, Lorrie, to the meeting on Sunday evening. They attended that night, and the service began with a restatement of our theme and a brief exhortation to repent.

This was followed by a testimony from a diminutive woman who had once been demonized. She told the audience about a frightening experience she had had in the basement of her church. While teaching Sunday school one morning, she had a violent demonic manifestation. Children ran in terror as she hurled six-foot tables across the room and screamed profanities. Six men eventually subdued her. She was then taken to a Christian counselor who prayed for deliverance. The entire church sat in silence as she shared her story.

Jeff, the other pastor, then said by a word of knowledge, "I believe there are five women here who have throat-related problems. If you will come forward, we will pray for you now."[2] Five women came forward and lined up in a row. Jeff and I talked with one woman, while John and Lorrie ministered to another.

"Since these meetings began, I have been choking," said one woman. I felt prompted to ask her if she had suicide in her family. "Yes," she said, "my brother hung himself two weeks ago." We commanded the spirit of suicide to leave the woman. She manifested a brief tearful groan, then an obvious peace descended over her. The spirit left and the choking sensation stopped.

A few minutes later, John and I were ministering to a woman complaining of thyroid problems. As John interviewed her, she began to shake. Being somewhat buoyed by the first encounter, I prayed, "If there are any evil spirits in this woman, I demand you manifest now." This is not a prayer we should pray unless we are prepared for the consequences. Immediately, the woman began to groan and scream, as she shook violently. John prayed, "Evil spirit, in the name of Jesus, I command you to give us your name." "Lust," said a deep, guttural voice. "Lust, in the name of Jesus, I command you to leave this woman and never come back," John said. After a few more minutes of prayer, she was reasonably composed and able to return to her seat. She now leads a deliverance team in her church and has been a help to many.

There were several more people set free that evening, all within the space of an hour, and in the full view of the entire congregation. The experience of that evening gave me a healthy understanding of war with the devil.

What was happening? As people repented of their sins, the presence of Jesus came close to heal, save and deliver. It perhaps seems curious to us that there were so many demons in Jesus' day? Virtually absent in the Old Testament, they spring forth with vengeance in the gospels.

Demonic elements manifest themselves whenever the kingdom of God comes in power. The closer the kingdom comes, the more demons are exposed. They are not exposed by emotion, reason or even biblical content, but they are revealed in the presence of kingdom power. And so as we do the works of the kingdom, we are likely to bump into demons.

The Gerasene demoniac is the most dramatic story of a demonized person in the New Testament. While we are not likely to run into anyone like this, studying the account will help us understand spiritual warfare against demons.[3]

Prior to meeting the demoniac, Jesus and his disciples had encountered a fierce storm in the Sea of Galilee (Lk 8:22-25). Where did the storm come from? Was it just a disturbance to manifest Jesus' rule over nature? That may be one reason, but there is another. The storm was a *demonic assault sent to stop Jesus* as he came to rescue the demonized man. Demonic reconnaissance spotted Jesus on his way to help the man and tried to halt his progress.

If we minister to demonized people, storms will be thrown in our paths also. We may find our bodies and emotions are attacked with sickness and depression. We may see our families come under attack through accidents and financial difficulty. We may see our church torn apart by internal strife and hostility. But we are not powerless in the face of these attacks. We have authority in Jesus' name over demons and disease, and we also have authority to rebuke the storms the enemy throws in our way to stop us (Mt 10:1). *We must learn to rebuke the storms; then we rebuke demons face-to-face.*

Demons do not remain quiet for long (Lk 8:28-29). During his torment, the Gerasene was naked, chained in tombs, under armed guard, escaping and running wild in the desert, crying out with a loud voice and generally scaring everyone to death. I have been in meetings when several demonized people were all manifesting at the same time. It is not a pretty sight and can be terribly frightening. However, we need not be disturbed. Such occurrences do happen in kingdom ministry and seem to be particularly present in certain revivals.[4]

The classic response of demonized people is a violent reaction to the presence of the Holy Spirit, to the name of Jesus, or to the mention of the cross and Christ's blood. The reaction may include fleeing, flopping, flipping, foaming or fighting. The person may experience their eyes rolling back in their head, localized pain, chills, violent shaking or sudden sleepiness, or they may begin speaking in threatening voices and uttering profanity.

When Jesus climbed ashore, "he was met by a demon-possessed man" (Lk 8:26-27). The word *met* can refer either to meeting a friend or a foe. Interestingly, this was the dilemma of the demoniac. One side of him was repelled by Jesus and made him want to run, while the other side was drawn to Jesus because he knew there was hope.

Demons will incite people to run and fight, while the victims simultaneously will be aware that deliverance is their only hope. This will produce in them a love/hate relationship with those who pray for them. In this ministry, people's will to resist the flight-and-fight response is most important. They must choose to be released from demonic bondage, be broken before God and repent of any sin. We cannot help anyone who does not ultimately want our help.

Jason was a transvestite male who manifested numerous demons. Several of us prayed for him, but made little progress. Jason had become familiar with his spirits and was unwilling to live without them. He was afraid he would have no personality if these alien forces left.

Tim, a young pastor with a growing ministry, handled his demonization very differently. Several demons had invaded his life through persistent pornography. They laid claim to Tim and convinced him he would soon participate in child abuse and homosexuality. Yet Tim knew Jesus could set him free if he was willing to repent. During one twenty-four-hour period, Tim was set free, primarily out of his own determination to persist until God delivered him.

How Demonization Occurs

The Gerasene man who met Jesus is described as being "demon-possessed" (Lk 8:27). Evangelicals, in an effort to describe what can happen to Christians versus non-Christians, have developed various categories such as "oppression by demons" and "possession by demons." The most frequently used terms in the New Testament are "having demons" *(echōn daimonia)* and the participle "demonized" *(daimonizomai)*. Francis Mac-Nutt helps elucidate these terms:

> *Daimonizomai* is better translated in the broader sense of "demon influenced" than in the narrow sense of "demon possessed." The problem is in the term "possession." Real possession, when an individual's personality is submerged by an alien evil force, is certainly rare. It is nothing most of us need be concerned about. But the word in the New Testament which is often translated as "possessed" actually means . . . something like "demonized," which is a broader term. I find that possession is rare, but people who are "demonized" or attacked or oppressed by demonic forces are a relatively common occurrence.[5]

Can Christians be demonized? Can their lives, in some fashion, be influenced by the demonic? Although this question is hotly debated, I think the answer is *yes*.[6] Such assaults can be involuntary or voluntary.

Involuntary demonization comes through heredity, curses or traumatic events. Psychiatrist Kenneth McAll tells the story of a clergyman whose daughter was hospitalized for wanting to gouge out the eyes of her children. When the priest began to examine his family tree, he found this obsession in his lineage for many generations. When he decided to celebrate the Eucharist over his daughter and to break the *hereditary curse*, the daughter was completely healed. He later found out that an aunt in another mental hospital was healed at the very same moment. The demons which had ruled the family had been dismissed.[7]

Such curses do not only come from the occult or witchcraft. A curse can be placed on someone through repeated verbal condemnation by a parent or authority figure.

Becky was a young married woman who had come to me with her husband for counseling. After a thirty-minute interview, I began to pray for her in the presence of her husband. We prayed for about thirty minutes before the Lord spoke to me. He told me to break a curse over Becky, a curse placed on her by the verbal abuse of her father and mother. With each word I pronounced to break its power, Becky writhed in emotional pain. There were over a dozen words her parents had spoken over her which functioned as curses, words of slander and accusation, initiated by the enemy and uttered through the lips of her parents. That night the curses were broken and the enemy's assault stopped. But it took Becky time to get over the emotional scars which were left.

Unusual, traumatic events can also cause demonization. The enemy uses these moments of terror and trauma to invade a person, exploiting their weakness.

Debbie was held at gunpoint on two occasions, and raped on one. These traumas opened the way for demonic invasion. Debbie became terrorized about leaving her house and was unable to function in her role as a pastor's wife.

Debbie came to a healing seminar where no one knew of her background. Shortly after the prayer time began, she started to shake, and in a matter of minutes, fell on the floor. Normally, when this happens it is best to provide a private place for counsel so that no embarrassment comes to the person. Before she could be taken out of the room, however, she began to curse the pastor who was praying for her. By this time a crowd had gathered to observe the power encounter, reminiscent of the days of Jesus. Unemotionally, the pastor said to the group, "This woman has several evil spirits. Evil spirits cannot dwell where the light and love of God are present. Let's pray that the love of God will come on this woman right now."

As we prayed, Debbie responded with greater violence and profanity. But within a few minutes, after the pastor prayed several prayers commanding and dismissing the spirits, they left. Debbie got up a free woman. For months she told anyone who would listen about her deliverance. She was a member of a sexual abuse class, and the group became her primary avenue of evangelism. And Debbie was no longer housebound; she again was able to resume her duties with her husband.

Demonization can also come through voluntary means, such as habitual sin. Willful and continual sin opens a door for the devil. Satan can now give a power assist to the sin, taking the area entirely out of people's control. The problem has moved from the ordinary sphere of habitual sin which can be changed by repentance and self-discipline (Mt 3:8; 2 Pet 1:6) into one of demonic control. Although such people may have full choice-making ability in other areas of their life, in this area of continual sin they can no longer stop the action or thought. Counseling and resisting temptation are not enough to break the bondage at this point.

Occult involvement can also be a means of voluntary demonization. This includes even experimentation with occult practices, such as fortune telling and ouija boards. It also applies to anyone who has made an outright invitation to demons or the devil. Some Christians, in times of loneliness and depression, have made pacts with the enemy. These invitations must be renounced and all access doors closed.

Many believers who have had occult involvements have never fully repented at their confession of faith and baptism. These baptismal candidates need to make a full renunciation of all demonic forces before baptism. Otherwise, they might be starting their Christian walks with areas of their lives not fully given over to God; this can hamper them the rest of their lives. All believers should confess and repent for any occult practices which may have been part of their personal or family histories (Jas 5:16).

Levels of Demonization

Demonization occurs at different levels and to different degrees. Figure 1 visualizes this variation.[8]

Each of the four quadrants represents a degree of control and a degree of manifestation by the demonic. *All four quadrants could equally be called demonization.* Quadrant 1 represents the level of *oppression.* This is where the devil is sifting, tempting or attacking a believer. Job is the classic Old Testament example of oppression. New Testament examples are when Jesus rebuked the demonic activity in Peter, and when Satan wanted to sift Peter (Mt 16:22-23; Lk 22:31-32). The temptation of all believers by the devil fits into this section as the most elementary level of demonization.

Quadrant 2 is the section of *infestation.* The devil now has a partial foothold in a person. There is some level of control and some degree of manifestation. Several examples apply here: the "daughter of Abraham," whom Satan had bound for eighteen long years (Lk 13:10-17); Satan's filling of the hearts of Ananias and Sapphira so they lied to the Holy Spirit (Acts 5:1-11); the Corinthian believer who was delivered over to Satan because of his sexual immorality (1 Cor 5:5), and Hymenaeus and Philetus who had gone astray in their teaching and were now in the snare of the devil, held captive to do his will (2 Tim 2:14-26).

Quadrant 3 represents *partial control.* The degree and manifestation have increased from quadrant 2, but a measure of personal control re-

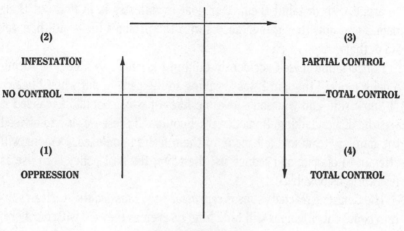

OFTEN MANIFESTED

(2)

INFESTATION

NO CONTROL — — — — — — — — — — — — — — — — — —TOTAL CONTROL

(1)

OPPRESSION

(3)

PARTIAL CONTROL

(4)

TOTAL CONTROL

SELDOM MANIFESTED

mains. Possible New Testament examples are the boy with the convulsive demon (Lk 9:37-40), the demonized mute man (Mt 9:32-33) and the daughter of the Syrophoenician woman (Mk 7:24-30).

Quadrant 4 is about *total control* at all times, and full manifestations at all times. Our best biblical example is the Gerasene demoniac (Lk 8:26-39). I expect there are many of these people today in North America—perhaps those who are sedated in mental hospitals, or who roam the streets, homeless.

Deliverance

Although the Gerasene demoniac fell in the presence of Jesus (for demons do bow in his presence), there was still a battle going on (Lk 8:28-29). The demons begged Jesus not to torment them by sending them into the abyss of hell. Mark's Gospel indicates that the man was also rebuking Jesus, imploring the name of God against him (Mk 5:7). The demoniac seemed to recognize Jesus' authority at the same time he was struggling to escape the punishment which that authority could order. Demons don't give in easily, even if they know they are defeated. We are never to argue with or taunt them. Our goal in ministry is to find out their names and how they gained access into the person's life—and then get rid of them.

I once found myself accidently talking too much to a demon during a deliverance. I thought I was speaking to the person, but when I heard, "I know you, and you don't love me like a pastor should!" I realized it was the demon talking. Immediately, I could tell these words had divided the ministry team and left many of them feeling confused. Demons will attempt to distract and seduce us; therefore, the best policy is to use as few words as possible.

The Gerasene reacted as Jesus *repeatedly commanded* the unclean spirit to come out.[9] Demons will hide from us even as they did with our Lord, but eventually they must come out. Jesus was not an exorcist, in the sense that he did not use incantations and long prayers over the demonized. Jesus was a "demon-expulser," casting out demons with a word.[10] Ministry to the demonized is not marked by emotion or physical force; it is done with the authority of Jesus' name, relying upon him to back us up.

When asked his name, the demoniac responded "Legion," because he had many demons (Lk 8:30-34). In those times, a Roman legion consisted of 5,000-6,000 troops. Mark 5:13 says that there were about 2,000 pigs on the hill. This gives us some idea of how thoroughly demonized this man must have been.

The demons did not want to go to the abyss, the burning pit of imprisoned spirits, so they begged Jesus to let them go into a large herd of swine grazing on a nearby hillside. Jesus gave them permission to do so, and as soon as the demons went into the pigs, they went crashing down the hill into the lake and drowned. This gives us a graphic idea of the destructive intent of demons. Deliverance ministry works best when the following guidelines are followed:[11]

First, we need to discern the presence of demonic activity. Those who have the gift of "distinguishing between spirits" are indispensable on a team ministering to the demonized (1 Cor 12:10). God uses this gift of spiritual discernment to reveal the presence of evil spirits. Ways in which evil can be discerned include: a felt sense of evil, sighting a spirit on a person, or smelling an odor of demons.

Second, we want to explain the principle of personal responsibility. This is one of the ground rules that the person we are praying for must understand. We tell them, "Christ can set you free, but you must be willing to be free." Next, we explain how the person must honestly work with us and the Holy Spirit, avoiding any lack of cooperation.

Third, we lead them in repenting of their sins. If the person has not yet received Christ, we lead them in repenting of their sins, accepting Christ as Lord and Savior, and we invite the Holy Spirit to fill them. If the person is a Christian, we ask them to confess any sins they have not yet repented for, either now or whenever they become aware of it in the prayer process. In both cases, we pronounce them forgiven according to James 5:16 after they have confessed.

Fourth, in Jesus' name, we demand that the spirit identify itself. We can then break the power of the stronghold, and close off access points to the person's life. We command the spirits to leave. We will want to pray for the protection of the person and the team, and for the peaceable exit of the spirit. At all times we want to treat the person with supreme dignity, for our highest calling is to minister in love. Therefore, we will keep a soft edge on our language, separating our speaking to the demon from our speaking to the person. During the procedure, we must be sensitive to God's leading, saying only what the Spirit is saying. We maintain constant eye contact with the demonized person, since the eye is a window of the spirit and gives us a good idea about what is happening in the person (Mt 6:22).

Fifth, it should be very clear when the spirit has left. If we are sure we are dealing with an evil spirit and not just an emotional disorder, then we will be just as certain when the evil spirit has left—and so will the person we are praying for.

The healing of the demoniac restored health to the Gerasene man, brought fear of God to the people, and inspired the proclamation of the gospel throughout the entire city (Lk 8:35-39). We should look for similarly godly results when we bring Jesus' freedom to those who are oppressed by Satan. When we minister in love and exercise the spiritual authority Jesus has given us, health and holiness are brought to the church—two qualities desperately needed in the body of Christ today.

III War in the Church

7 Watch Out for Hungry Lions

WHEN JIMMY CARTER BECAME PRESIDENT OF THE UNITed States, an Air Force general promptly came into the Oval Office to explain the procedure for evacuating the chief executive in cases of emergency. The general informed Carter that it would take less than five minutes to get him out of the White House and winging toward safety.

"Okay," said the president. "*Go!*"

"Go?" asked the general incredulously.

"That's right," said Carter. "Go!"

The general turned pale and scrambled into action. Aides scurried about. Phones rang. Carter went back to work. Forty-five minutes later, as the general was still shouting orders into a telephone, Carter calmly asked, "Got the time, General?"

In spiritual warfare, it is easy to assume we are prepared. But when the test comes and the enemy launches an attack on us, we may find that we are not ready at all. Precious time will be lost if we are not prepared to respond immediately with a set plan.

One realm of warfare which may take us by surprise is warfare within the church. It's painful to admit that the church should be an arena for warfare, but it is; and we must be willing to acknowledge that if we want to fight where the battle is raging. The next five chapters will look at various forms of warfare within the church.

This chapter focuses on 1 Peter 5:1-11. This letter begins with a call for leaders to shepherd their flocks with proper attitudes and ethics. Seven commands are given which are intended to prevent conflict in the church. Peter also addresses the source of these conflicts—the enemy, who Peter depicts as an opponent and as a lion.

Our Enemy, Our Opponent

The word used for *enemy* in 1 Peter 5:8 suggests an opponent in a lawsuit. Picture this: Our enemy has brought an accusation against us, and now he wants to sue; he wants to take everything which is rightfully ours. He wants to tie us up in spiritual litigation, so we have no time for the kingdom of God. *He wants to keep us reactive to his assaults, rather than proactive for God's agenda.*

This is the enemy's, the opponent's, desire. And when he launches these kinds of attacks from within the church, it can leave us stunned and hurt. Consider the story of Pete, a pastor who was boldly following God's leading for revival.

Pete was a bright, energetic pastor of a popular denominational church. Somewhat accidentally, he stumbled into a ministry of bringing renewal to his tradition. Initially his contributions were tolerated by his elders. But then their response turned hostile.

Confused by their negative reaction, Pete became depressed and suffered a strong sense of rejection. Soon, unfounded rumors began to circulate that he was a homosexual; he and his wife were shunned by their friends; Pete was dismissed from his church and soon after defrocked by his denomination. The effects of this ordeal hung over Pete and his wife for years.

Pete was not the only one hit hard: the once-prosperous church lost over five hundred members, as believers fought each other over decisions to be made. The matter was released to the press, whose weekly accounts of the church's shame kept the community informed for months. Not surprisingly, the elders of the church became bitter and scattered throughout the city. Several of them quit going to church at all.

Today, Pete is in another city, and has a healthy ministry. He has been vindicated by most of his former critics. But for years, the enemy was allowed to wage his accusations, tie up the church in confusion and halt any advancement for the kingdom.

In Pete's case, the opponent got away with his hurtful scheme for years. Pete *was* largely out of commission in his work for God's kingdom, and it took him and his wife years of therapy to get over the hurt and confusion they felt. But we can learn from Pete's ordeal, and head off the enemy before opposition robs us of our rightful place in God's service.

Our Enemy the Lion

The next image Peter gives in his letter is of a "roaring lion looking for someone to devour" (v. 8). The image is apropos. We will look at several ways in which Satan's attack on us, in the church, is very much like a lion on the prowl.

Like a lion, Satan is constantly on the move. The devil and his demons are not omnipresent like God, so they must move about to do their evil work. At times they are very close; and then they leave again to attack some other person, in some other place.

As he moves about, the enemy may launch a *subtle attack*, particularly of temptation, which may last for a few minutes or a few hours and then be gone. *Prolonged attacks* may last for weeks, a more profound *siege* may last for years.

There are a number of ways we can come to recognize the enemy's ploys in our lives. Some key areas are his favorite to attack, and we will look at how the enemy likes to stir things up.

Opposition at work. Things at work may not be going quite right. For no particular reason, people aren't responding to us well. We examine our behavior and attitudes, to be sure we are acting in grace and honesty. Yet we find ourselves halted at every step. We may get fired or passed over for promotions. Financially, things at home are getting tight.

Conflict in the family. Every family has its Achilles' heel which the devil will exploit. But there are also seasons when even the best of families are besieged with disproportionate and hostile conflicts. Despite everyone's efforts, no one is getting along with anyone else.

Opposition before or after an outreach for the kingdom. For me, this usually comes in the form of sickness, emotional distress or some major trauma in my church. One year, however, the attack was on my family.

My parents had traveled to Canada to be present at my daughter's thirteenth birthday. This was a big occasion, and we had looked forward to the trip by "MaMa and PaPa." Their trip also happened to precede a weekend conference I was to do for the Christian Medical Society.

The night before my daughter's birthday, in the wee hours of the morning, my parents had a strange visitation. A dragon-shaped figure appeared in their bedroom. My mother, not understanding what was happening, mistook this as a sign they were to leave. As we talked in the early hours of the morning, I assured her that it was spiritual warfare, and that occurrences often came prior to ministry times. We simply rebuked the enemy, affirmed we were not changing our plans, and would not be led into fear by his tactics.

The conference was significant for many doctors, giving them a new perspective on their medical practice and the advancement of the kingdom. And my parents' visit was important for my daughter. From time to time my mother still asks, "Are you sure there was a dragon on the wall?" I assure her that there certainly was, and I remind her that the enemy resorts to all kinds of tactics to keep us from doing God's work.

Unusual spiritual dryness. We feel like our prayers do not get beyond the ceiling, and our Bible reading seems like meditating on the classified ads. We are dry, dry, dry, and there is no refreshment at hand.

Heightened temptations. Areas of temptation long laid to rest now raise their ugly heads with a vicious resurgence. This is a pretty clear sign that a lion is roaming near our home.

Satan the hungry lion wants to devour us like a meal. Besides being a prowler, he has a vicious appetite. In 1 Peter 5:8, the term *devour* means to swallow whole. Jesus uses the term when he describes the Pharisees as those who "strain out gnats, but swallow camels" (Mt 23:24). In the Old Testament, we see it used when Jonah is swallowed by the big fish (Jon 1:17), and when Pharaoh's army is covered by the sea (Ex 15:5). The enemy wants to attack us, rip us apart, and ferociously devour us whole.

The devil is not interested in bartering for small portions of our lives; he wants it all. I remember praying for a Bible college student who, in a fit of rebellion, asked Satan to heal her of a particular physical ailment. To her surprise, she was healed instantaneously. But then she began to realize that the intention of the enemy was not to do her a good deed and then leave, but to devour her entire life, using the doorway she had opened to him.

As the devil moves about, he makes lots of terrifying noises. The enemy would like to scare us. But once we learn his tricks, we can also learn to quiet him in Jesus' name.

I received a phone call one day, long before I had begun to witness demonic manifestations. "Pastor," said the British-sounding woman, "I believe I have a demon, and I need help."

Not knowing any better at the time, and assuming she was just a little weird, I began to demythologize her supposed demonic experience. Halfway into my reasoned argument, I was interrupted by a shrill, strong voice on the other end of the line. I had never heard anything like it before. It scared me so badly that the hair on the back of my neck stood up.

Demonized people can make some horrible noises, but in Jesus' name they can be silenced (Lk 4:35).

Like a hungry lion, the enemy seeks out the weak for his next meal. Who are the devil's prey, those picked-off with little trouble? They are the ones who do not know they are being pursued. They are unaware that a battle is going on; they don't know there is danger in playing with sin. They are the ones who do not run when the enemy comes with temptation, and they quickly give up when the fight begins.

In his letter, Peter gives four profiles which are most vulnerable to the attack of the prowling lion: the proud, the anxious, the sleepy and the passive (1 Pet 5:5, 7, 8, 9).

The Proud Are Vulnerable

The proud are the first target of the enemy (1 Pet 5:5). God is looking for humble men and women. Therefore, the enemy delights in those who hold on to their pride.

Peter advises young men to be submissive to their elders—but God opposes (literally, is anti-submissive to) the proud. We submit to God by clothing ourselves with humility, even as Jesus dressed himself in humble attire to wash the disciples' feet (Jn 13:1-15).

Humility is both an attitude and an action. Paul illustrates this distinction in his letter to the Philippians (Phil 2:3, 8). In verse 3, humility is an attitude, disciplined by selfless love and devotion to the interest of others. We are to "consider others better than ourselves." It is not denigrating self-talk, but God-talk which elevates the estimation of others. Verse 8 reveals humility as not only lowliness of mind, but lowliness in action. Humbling oneself means volunteering to serve, taking orders and fitting into the arrangements of others.

One church in the Midwest, trying to manifest the essence of this passage, expresses humility in its adherence to four standards. First, they pray by night and day. Their primary intention is not marathon praying, but to humbly recognize that God's strength builds the church, not man's. Second, they value holiness of heart. This standard recognizes God's order for life, as opposed to man's. Third, they practice extravagant giving. They humble themselves to God's superior purposes for their resources. Practically, this means each staff family lives with a minimum salary and simple accommodations. Fourth, this church demonstrates an unwavering faith. God's provisions are always regarded as superior to man's.

The virtue of humility is essential; God cannot find it in his nature to bless those who are not humble. Being humble is being childlike. This quality is the goal of our Christian life.

Pride is just the opposite in attitude and action. It is arrogant and haughty in the way it assesses itself, and it's judgmental in its regard for others. With this mental approach, it is impossible to be of service to anyone else. The proud person is unsubmissive to God, devoid of the Spirit's filling, and often conflicts with others in the body of Christ.

The latter half of the 1980s revealed the shame of immoral television evangelists and pastors. As the media paraded these men before us, it became obvious that their problems exceeded the lust of their loins; their attitudes and actions were out of line with God. These men were proud.

Pride truly goes before destruction (Prov 16:18). What happened to those ministers could easily happen to us; we are all susceptible to pride that leads us down foolish paths. As my friend Paddy Ducklow says, "You can either choose to humble yourself, or be humiliated. The choice is up to you." Humility is our grace covering, protecting us from the enemy. To step out of humility and into pride is to invite the devil to eat us alive.

The Anxious Are at Risk

The anxious are the next group vulnerable to the enemy's attack (1 Pet 5:7). This wrong attitude leaves us open to the enemy's attack.

Though we cannot simply dismiss the troubled circumstances that make us anxious, we can do something about how we respond. We can refuse to be robbed of the confidence that God is near. The root of the word *anxiety* means "to divide"; indeed, anxiety divides our attention and distracts us from full devotion. We cannot fully obey God because we are not fully trusting him. We rely on our own efforts and question if God is really in the picture at all. We then cry out to him for help, but doubt his ability to come to our aid. So we are back where we started, trying to handle everything ourselves.

It has been said that anxiety is misplaced imagination. It may be more accurate to say that it is the devil's imagination, sold to us as reality. Whenever we bear the burden for what rightly belongs to God, the enemy has a field day.

Anxiety appears to have two bases: threat and pride. As threat, *anxiety is our experience of psychological defensiveness.* Two people can experience the same events and respond in entirely different manners. Therefore, anxiety is not dependent on our circumstance, but on our internal response to it. Something external triggers a reaction which disturbs our equilibrium.

While driving on a freeway, Carl saw a car in the next lane. One of the men in the car was wearing a strange mask. This made Carl anxious, and he steered clear of them. Other drivers saw the same scene and laughed, thinking it must be a joke. Same event, very different responses.

Where do these internal threats come from? Some psychologists suggest they come from *parents and authority figures who have failed us.* Naively, we entered the world believing that larger people would nurture and care for us. But then we discover that the opposite is true—for some, because they have been sexually abused. External pain and internal confusion propel anxiety in the child. Trusting is no longer possible. Defending one's territory becomes uppermost.

Anxiety can also be produced in ways not so apparently brutal, but still harmful. A parent may become anxious because the child is not living up to their internal standards. For example, the child dresses in a manner which the parent feels is sloppy and dirty. The parent begins, in both overt and covert ways, to point out the child's impropriety. Because of the parent's authority and the constant dose of correction, the child appropriates his parent's standard so that the parent will not be anxious. After the child has grown, however, he continues to carry this anxiety, and becomes an anxious adult.

Anxiety can also come from *events or patterns which have transpired in our lives.* Falling from a horse could produce anxiety about riding; falling from a ladder could promote a fear of heights. Repeated patterns, like confronting a demeaning elementary-school teacher everyday, could produce physical and emotional anxiety. This could manifest itself in headaches, stomach cramps, bed-wetting, lying, crying and uncontrolled anger.

Another reason we feel anxious is simply because of the presence of sin in the world. Because we are tarnished by Adam's sin, we are defensive against our own Maker. We find it impossible to believe he loves us and has our best interests at heart (1 Jn 4:16). No matter how many times we hear it and repeat it to others, we are suspicious about his fidelity.

Watching from the sidelines, the devil will exploit every angle of anxiety. The abusive parent, the demeaning teacher, the tragic Fall—they all become venues for his work.

We also find that anxiety has a base in our pride, a *self-imposed pressure to keep things moving by our own efforts.* This may show up in ways we wouldn't normally think of as being prideful, but evidence of pride is in our belief that we have control.

For me, anxiety rooted in pride showed up in, of all places, an amusement park. The children talked me into riding a gondola which ran the length of Expo 86, about seventy-five feet off the ground. Now this was no small feat, since I suffer from a fear of heights. One of our family rules is the "terra firma" principle, which I invoke whenever we go to fairgrounds and carnivals. I simply decline any amusement ride I do not like with the phrase, "The more firma I have, the less terra I feel." I was fine when I got onto the gondola that day, and as long as it kept moving I was okay. But without warning, our glass carriage stopped right over a large body of water. For hours—or so it seemed—we hung in space, balancing on a wire no wider than a broomstick. When we eventually reached the other side, the children had a good laugh: my hands had sweated so badly that drops of water had fallen on my light-colored pants in a most inappropriate place. I was suffering from an anxiety attack, a self-imposed pressure to keep our gondola in the air.

Anxiety is the hairline crack in the armor of pride. Panic sets in once we realize we can't keep everything together. Anxiety is the emotional defeat of pride and should act as an alarm for our spiritual life. We are not all-sufficient. We really do need God to come to our aid. When anxiety overtakes us, it is a good time to humble ourselves before him.

Defeating pride means trusting someone else with our destiny and life. There are three questions we can ask anxious people to help them get to this point. First, "Is there someone who is powerful enough to be called upon for help?" Assuming that they have answered "God," we proceed to the second question: "Can we trust God to handle our lives in a way which has our best interest at heart?" Last, the emotional question: "Are we worthy to be helped?"

Each of these questions strikes at the heart of a personal relationship with a personal Redeemer. At each question the devil would like to impose his own answers; "No, he is not there! No, he is not to be trusted! And you are unworthy of his help!" When we believe Satan's lies, the torment of anxiety remains with us.

So how can we handle anxiety and hold off the damage of the enemy?

Name our anxiety. We need to get a grip on what is at the center of our worry, what fear is plaguing our steps. Vague feelings won't do; we need to be as specific as possible.

Talk to ourselves. Although rational arguments do not usually cause anxiety to disappear, they at least let us see the irrational side of what we are saying and believing. We can say with Mark Twain, "I am an old man and have known a great many troubles, but most of them never happened."

Receive personal prayer. We need several people who can pray effective personal prayers to minister God's healing to us. We need people who have a sense of the source of our problem, why it reoccurs, and how the Holy Spirit wants to heal and deliver us.

Trusting relationships. By God's allowance, we need to build trusting relationships with several people. New patterns are needed to blot out old memories.

Renounce our pride. We need to admit our inadequacy. We cannot carry the responsibility alone for everything in our lives.

Remind ourselves of Scripture. What words has God given us about our future, our health, our finances and our importance to him? We then need to confess these words back to God, agreeing with him on the subject. This gives us a proper perspective on our lives.

Persevere. Freedom from anxiety will come as we carry on in life, following the promises of Scripture, and accepting the healing God has for us.

Practice praise. We need to rejoice in the Lord, relaxing in his care and protection, specifically giving each anxiety over to him in prayer (Phil 4:4-6).

The Passive Are an Easy Target

Those who are spiritually unalert and passive are easy prey for the enemy. They never see him coming, and when he attacks, they hardly know what hit them.

The sleepy-headed are vulnerable to the attack of the enemy (1 Pet 5:8). These are the ones who go to sleep and cannot pray against temptation (Mt 26:41). They are the ones whose bodies and emotions overrun their spirits. It is spiritual drowsiness that is unaware of the surrounding dynamics. It is a father who does not know his lack of communication is affecting his children. It is the wife who ignores the legitimate sexual needs of her husband. It is the sleepy-headed pastor who fails to realize his congregation has lost its first love (Rev 2:4).

Although the exhortation to alertness is usually concerning the Second Coming of Jesus (Mk 13:33-37), it is also used to focus on incoming assaults of the enemy. We are to be free of any form of mental drunkenness, excessive passions or rash behavior. We are to be wide awake to everything transpiring around us.

If we had asked Andy about his marriage, he would have said everything was fine. But Sharon, his wife of ten years, did not feel the same. She continually gave signals of her unhappiness and pled for a richer marital life. But Andy kept his head in the sand, playing the absentee husband. One day Sharon locked the door and told him never to come back. This shocked Andy awake, but it was too late. Sharon found someone else. Remember: the enemy picks off the sleepy-headed. Andy was not paying attention, he was not in the ball game, and the devil got one by him.

The lion can only devour what he has overtaken, or what has purposely lain down. Passive acceptance of our circumstances or our sin is permission for the devil to take more ground. The passive man or woman is a person who has lost all hope that any effort will make a difference.

The passive wife will stand by silently while the abusive husband molests her children. Not only does she fear intervening, but she reasons it would do no good. Nothing will change. The passive husband has lost all hope that his diligence at work will ensure a promotion or that his efforts with his family will gain him more respect. The alcoholic and drug addict have taken the passive route to solve their internal pain, the avenue of anesthesia. The homosexual in his passivity resists the notion of change and pleads the case of genetics. The teen-ager, sensing enormous failure, ends his life in suicide.

In each case, the will of the person is surrendered to the circumstance, to someone else, or to something else. This is not demonization, but it is similar to it. As a result of the Fall, man suffered a "bondage of the will." In Christ, man is restored to choice-making ability, with a power assist toward righteousness. Yet if a believer surrenders his will to someone else or to some substance, God cannot freely move in his life. Our wills, cooperating with God's disposition toward holiness, can keep us from the devil's bondage.

Lois is "too Christian" to ever be angry outwardly, but on the inside she is a boiling pot of rage. Whenever she comes for counseling, she is tempted to reveal what she truly feels. But as soon as she does, she backpedals, and denies the reality of her feelings. Lois is passive. By denial she covers up her real self. In her passivity she refuses to wrestle with the ugly and painful parts of her past. Although God would help her get through it, Lois refuses to fight. God will not heal what we refuse to reveal.

Passivity toward the devil is to be replaced by active resistance (1 Pet 5:9). A friend taught me a little exercise to demonstrate the principle of resistance. I have someone stand in front of me with their arms and hands extended outward. We then grasp hands together and I tell them to "resist" my pushing. At first, I catch them off guard and can easily push them over. They are not actively resisting. Then they learn that resisting means pushing back with their entire strength. That's what it's like in spiritual warfare: resisting the enemy by pushing him back with a determined spiritual effort.

We all need to know how to resist the enemy, because spiritual warfare is common to all believers (1 Pet 5:9). In fact, the hotter the spiritual environment we are in, the more intense will be the opposition. The devil's ultimate desire is for us to leave the faith through the strains he places upon us. But God, because of his grace, has pledged to war with us in this battle (1 Pet 5:10).

Notice the promises God makes to us in verse 10. He will come and restore us in our battle position, he will make us "strong, firm and steadfast." The word *restore* is related to the word *prepare* in Ephesians 4:12, and both words carry the sense that God is giving us the tools to complete the warfare. In the Greek translation of the Old Testament, the word *enable* from Psalm 18:33 also conveys this meaning: "He makes my feet like the feet of a deer; he enables me to stand on the heights." Although the battle is real and intense, God supplies the tools and makes us strong enough to get the job done. He makes us firm in our position and lays a foundation which cannot be shaken. Jesus is the foundation, and he has poured his very life into us, a life which is able to protect us from the most merciless opponent and the most vicious lion.

8 Enemies of Unity

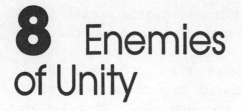

WHAT JESUS BEGAN WITH TWELVE DISCIPLES AND NU-merous followers has become a worldwide phenomenon, splintered into over 20,000 separate denominations. In 1979, the Center for the Study of World Evangelization in Nairobi produced a computerized survey of world Christianity. Its research concluded: "Of all Christians, 1,323,390,000 are church members affiliated to . . . 20,780 distinct Christian denominations across the world."[1]

The existence of over 20,000 separate denominations bears witness to a remarkable spread of the gospel. Geographical and cultural boundaries have been penetrated by the Word of God. People groups have taken on their own Christian culture and spoken relevantly, not with a foreign tongue, to the peoples of their world. Denominations have preserved ethnic identities, and allowed traditions to emphasize aspects of the gospel which have been ignored by others. They have allowed churches to pool their resources to build schools, hospitals and to plant more churches. The story of 20,000 denominations also includes much to be ashamed of. There are traditions which are so provincially focused that they cannot acknowledge the genuine work of God in others. Numerous church splits have peppered the church's history. It takes little provocation for Christians to square off against each other like the Hatfields and the McCoys, leaving one another bruised and bleeding before the watching world. Separating from one another takes little or no effort—it is the natural consequence of walking in the flesh rather than in the Spirit (Gal 5:16-24). It takes enormous energy, however, for believers to dwell in unity.

Why should we be concerned for the unity of the church? The answer lies in the great comfort and assurance of being one with the people of God. We are not alone in our battle with the enemy. We are not so crazy after all, for over one billion of us on planet earth believe the message of redemption through God's Son. United, we begin to sense we are an invincible army, moving to repossess the territory Satan stole in the garden. We are God's remnant people, assured of victory and destined to spend eternity with one another. It feels good to stand shoulder-to-shoulder and to march along the path of worship in truth.

This unity is what God desires for every church. And as we know, what God desires to build, Satan desires to destroy. In this chapter we will look at unity and the enemies of unity as they are discussed in the epistle of James. We will see that spiritual warfare has a suprapersonal side as well as a personal side.

Unity

How good and pleasant it is when brothers live together in unity! It is like precious oil poured on the head, running down on the beard, running down on Aaron's beard, down upon the collar of his robes. It is as if the dew of Hermon were falling on Mount Zion. For there the LORD bestows his blessing, even life forevermore. (Ps 133)

What mental picture did David have in mind when he penned these words? No doubt he intended them to be used in the processional pilgrim songs sung on the way to Jerusalem worship. The march up the hill of the Lord, with all the people of God, was baptized in unity. David pictures streams of people coming onto the main Jerusalem road, strangers from diverse towns and backgrounds, all joining in the processional with voices lifted in common praise.

In the psalm, David likens the unity of brothers and sisters to the precious oil poured upon Aaron at his ordination to the priesthood (Ex 29:7; Lev 8:12). Moving from his head to his beard, then to his collar and down upon his robe, he is anointed from head to foot.

What does this picture suggest for the church today? Unity is costly and not purchased cheaply; it is a delightful fragrance, able to be smelled by all those around. It also suggests the fluid work of the Holy Spirit, flowing down upon those who are worshipers of the one true and living God.

Such unity is not just expressed outwardly in gathered worship, but it is an inward reality in reconciled personal relationships. The East African revival, which is still going on, is a good example. As relationships were healed, brought into unity by mutual confession of sin and forgiveness, God worked powerfully to add millions to the church. One Ugandan bishop assured me, as he related the beginnings of the revival, that the unity of relationships was the primary moving force behind the awakening.

Most directly, I believe, the passage suggests that unity is our ordination to ministry. Covered from head to foot in unity, we acknowledge God's presence upon us and that he has set us for this task. Great leaders in the kingdom of God, such as Billy Graham and the late David Watson, have demonstrated this ordination of unity in their ministry, and the world has felt its impact. Walking in unity testifies to God's commissioning of us to do his work. Conversely, pride, suspicion and a standoffish posture point to our own desire to minister rather than to the call of God.

The second image in Psalm 133 is dew falling upon the mountains of Hermon and Zion. Hermon, at 9,232 feet, the highest mountain in ancient Israel, received the heaviest dew, about 250 days a year. Mount Zion, the lowest mountain, received a lighter dew, only 150 or so days of the year. This illustration confirms that both great and small are recipients of God's blessing; both great and small ministries need the blessing of unity. Small works of the kingdom usually crave the supportive unity of the body of Christ. Their resources are limited, their discouragement level is high and the sense of loneliness is ever present. By contrast, larger ventures in the kingdom are often too busy to think of the smaller ministries. But *both* ministries need the refreshment from heaven that unity can provide.

The psalm, in its use of the imagery of dew, also reminds us of Old and New Testament rain metaphors. Rain symbolizes those periods of unusual spiritual refreshment which fall on the people of God (Joel 2:23-32). This spiritual refreshment often characterizes seasons of revival, and it helps people work together. However, when there is no rain of refreshment, then we are even more in need of the dew of unity to keep us together. Both oil and dew are symbols of the presence of the Holy Spirit (Jas 5:13-16). If we want to find the manifestation of the Holy Spirit, then we need to look for genuine unity, for this is the gift of the Holy Spirit.

Unity does not originate with man, but flows from the heart of God. Three times in Psalm 133, the images reflect a down-flowing: unity flows down from above, from the hand of God. Now that he has given it to us, we must accept this gift and let it be manifested (Eph 4:3-6). Division is a great scandal in the church. When we fail to manifest God-given unity, we fail to represent God correctly to the people he loves.

"For there the LORD bestows his blessing, even life forevermore" (Ps 133:3). The "there" of this sentence has been variously suggested to be the family unit, or Jerusalem or the foot of Mount Zion. The grammatical antecedent is Zion, but the strength of the metaphor is unity. United, worshiping and singing on the road to Zion, there united under the anointed priestly garments, there united under the dew-soaked mountains, there is where the blessing of God abides. God blesses us as we walk in what he has given. Not only does he bless us with life forevermore, but with blessings in this life. The abolition of bitterness and resentment toward other believers brings the blessing of health. When churches cease to fight among themselves, we receive the blessing of living out a non-hypocritical gospel. Unity is God's blessing to the four billion who have yet to believe in Jesus Christ.

The Suprapersonal Side of Evil
In James 2—4, the author lists a series of characteristics which sound more like they belong to the pagan world than to the Christian. His list includes: bitter envy, selfish ambition, fights and quarrels, and curses and praises coming out of the same mouth (3:9-12, 14; 4:1). All of these destroy the unity of the church.

At first, we might be tempted to assign these characteristics to mere human nature, but James tells us that there is a *suprapersonal force* behind these characteristics (4:7). He says that bitter envy, selfish ambition, quarrels and conflicts, and speaking against one another come from " 'wisdom' [that] does not come down from heaven but is earthly, unspiritual, of the devil" (Jas 3:15). It is unspiritual, because it has not been influenced by the Spirit of God. It is wisdom which is demonic and motivated by Satan. James does not say that the problems come from personality conflicts, different visions or misunderstandings. He says it is an assault by the devil, manifested in conflicting relationships. There have been times when I, as a pastor, could have stood on my head, blown bubbles out my nose and sung "God Bless America," and I would not have pleased a particular group of people. Why? Because the devil was inciting them to riot, and they were unaware he was stirring them up. We don't want to give the devil undue credit, but we should charge him with those things he has earned. The problems James lists that Christians can fall prey to can be credited to the enemy.

Bitter Envy

The devil's first influence is seen in "bitter envy" (3:14). This is the only place in the New Testament where these two terms are combined and are variously translated as "harsh zeal," "rivalry" or "opinionatedness." Peter Davids says, "It is a zeal which can easily become blind fanaticism, bitter strife, or a disguised form of rivalry and thus jealousy. The person sees himself as jealous for truth, but others see bitterness, rigidity, and personal pride which are far from the truth."[2]

Barry had been a homosexual for over twenty years when he became a Christian and joined our fellowship. It was obvious he was serious about his faith and zealous to be a leader to others who were coming out of the same bondage. However, for various reasons, we passed over Barry for a leadership post. Eventually his jealousy became obvious to all. When Barry felt he could no longer influence our assessment, he turned and began to attack the pastoral team. Bitterness had replaced his zeal. Barry eventually left the church and looked for a place where he could lead. If we give the devil room to promote jealousy in our ranks, we can be assured he will use people like Barry to destroy the church.

The Bible has a positive use for the term *envy:* being zealous for God and his kingdom. In the Old Testament, Phinehas was zealous for the work of God and drove his spear through the heart of the adulterous Israelite and the Midianite woman (Num 25:1-17). A New Testament example is Jesus' cleansing of the temple. John attributes Jesus' cleaning out the merchandisers to a consuming zeal for God's temple to be a house of prayer (Jn 2:13-17).

Barry's mistake was that he had chosen to compete with brothers, when in reality the competition is with the devil. We need to throw all our energy into defeating his team, not picking off players on our side. Barry's zeal had been captured by a false motive, empowered by a deceiving spirit, and sent to do damage.

Selfish Ambition

The devil's influence is also seen in selfish ambition (Jas 3:14). This term describes rival leaders or a party spirit. "It is a spirit where jealous or angry leaders form a group which emotionally or physically withdraws from the rest of the church."[3] It was also the first temptation faced by the disciples (Mk 10:35-45).

Ambition is not in itself a bad quality. As with godly zeal, ambition is positively portrayed in the New Testament. We are to be ambitious for the work of God, but alert to the trap of being ambitious for our own ends. We must continually ask ourselves, "Who am I doing this for?" The object is not to become passive and back off from any moves of faith, but to be sure our ambitions are for what God wants to accomplish.

Webster defines *ambition* as a "strong desire for fame or power," and the willingness to "show great effort" to see this goal realized. The New Testament word for ambition could be literally translated "love of honor." It also carries the meanings "aspiration," "considering it an honor," and "having as one's ambition." The New Testament uses this word on three occasions, and the context for each is very instructive.

The first example, in 2 Corinthians 5:9, depicts ambition as expressing itself outwardly toward God, not inwardly for ourselves and our own honor. It is the love of his honor and a desire to please him which motivates us. Within this overall ambition to please God, Paul subsumes his next ambition, to preach Christ where he is not already named (Rom 15:20-21). Seeking the honor of God demands a priority of making him known where he is not known already. Our ambition is not first to find a church home for believers who are not being "fed," but rather to see non-Christians come to know Jesus and be enfolded into the church. The context of the third passage concerns the Second Coming of Jesus (1 Thess 4:11-12). Some of the Thessalonians were expecting it to happen any minute and so had abandoned a productive lifestyle as they waited for Jesus. Paul argues that brotherly love will compel us to be ambitious, not mooching off the church, but leading a productive and quiet life, working with our hands to provide our own living.

Biblical ambition can therefore be summarized as: 1) a desire to please God in all that we do; 2) a desire to proclaim his name where it is not known; and 3) a desire to engage in productive work whereby we can provide for our own needs and the needs of others.

Although this covers the New Testament treatment of this word, it does not resolve the conflict between our personal ambition and our ambition for God.

I am particularly sensitive to this issue because of years of harboring this sin in my own life. After my conversion, I was discipled by many men who are today leaders in the fundamentalist and evangelical communities. These men motivated me to study and work hard, and I am thankful for their model. Yet during those formative days, something else began to develop in my life: a desire to be a well-known and highly regarded Christian leader.

As I reflect upon it now, I realize that insecurities from my childhood made me vulnerable to this particular weakness. Unwittingly, much of my ministry was motivated by my own need. My ambition was born out of something more demanding than the love of God and service for his kingdom. In the last few years, however, God has been bringing me freedom in this area. I have had to learn how to refuse to be led by my personal ambition; I've had to call this sin *sin* and deny its right to control my life. God also ministered to me through inner healing from rejection. This gave me the freedom to please the Lord, and let the chips fall where they may when it came to pleasing people. And God graciously accepted me in my corrupt state, while he longed to give to me the motivation of Jesus.

Now that I am more aware of my own vulnerability, I can see this vice in other pastors. I see it in men who have no time to help another lonely pastor, and in pastors who can only talk about the size of their memberships and the expanse of their programs. We see it when a high-profile leader comes to town, and all the pastors begin to scramble to be known, to sit at the head table and be on the right committee. We see it in pompous dress and mannerisms which communicate competition. This behavior discourages unity and makes it impossible to prefer one another above ourselves and to work with one mind. At the same time, these same people long to be ambitious for God. They truly want to please him with all their lives and to seek his honor above their own. They *are* lovers of God—yet their hearts are still divided.

So how can we have the right kind of ambition, and do away with the selfish kind that destroys unity? These are a few guidelines that I have found helpful:

Freely admit to God and to ourselves that even in the best of times, our motivations for ministry are impure. Our motives will always have some sense of confusion, and the ability to separate them completely is not possible. "All a man's ways seem innocent to him, but motives are weighed by the LORD. Commit to the LORD whatever you do, and your plans will succeed" (Prov 16:2-3). We can thank God for looking upon our mixed motives and yet still loving and using us.

Confess to God the natural tendency for a self-directed love of honor. Acknowledge it as a sinful vice, not to be numbered among God's flock. Thank God we do not have to be bound by this vice any longer (Rom 6:6).

Ask God to reveal any hidden hurts which might be producing personal ambition. It is good to have a group of people pray for us about these hurts, and to ask God to bring us freedom.

Ask the Holy Spirit to fill and control our lives, particularly at this vulnerable point (Eph 5:18-20).

Begin to live a lifestyle of "confessing our sins to one another and praying for one another" (Jas 5:16). In this context, we may freely admit our failings and be open to exhortations from others. It is important to maintain a few close friendships with people who know us well enough to pray with us about our motives.

Agree with God about the rightness of biblical ambition. It is okay to want to please God by risk-taking ventures. It's okay to plant churches in places where Christ is not named. It's okay to work hard in ministry and provide for our family. It's okay to be ambitious for his honor.

If we do not have godly ambition, we need to ask God for the desire to fulfill his ambitions. Begin to plan and take the necessary steps for biblical ambition to be realized.

Last, seek to maintain a pure heart before God by reviewing these steps if ungodly ambition reappears.

Fights and Quarrels
After bitter envy and selfish ambition, the devil inspires fights and quarrels in the church (Jas 4:1). The Greek word for *fight* is used of wars in Luke 21:9, and the word for *quarrel* means a battle without weapons. These terms describe a situation where there is such hostility and tension that people are close to blows with one another. Here the devil has us on teams, projecting our brothers as the enemy. Time, energy and money are spent while we fight one another.

We have probably witnessed scenes like this: By congregational vote, the former pastor has been removed from the church, and now the church is trying to resolve who will be the next pastor. As the congregation enters the room, sides have already been formed. The smiles and lighthearted banter which characterized other meetings are absent. The discussion has little light, but lots of heat. Probably someone will end up angry and run out of the auditorium before the meeting is over. In fact, if it goes according to the devil's plan, someone will be saying in the back of their mind, "Hank, if you say that one more time, I'm going to knock your block off!" Meetings like this happen all the time. And each time they do, the enemy wins another victory. Some young Christian in the congregation will say, "Gee, if this is the church, I don't want to be part of it."

Speaking against One Another
Last, the devil inspires us to speak against one another (Jas 4:11-12).

When we speak against our brother or sister, we are vocalizing what is in our heart, because the mouth is the amplifier of the soul. The enemy sows a thought; that thought incubates until it is given birth in our speech. Once it is released, it mushrooms quickly. At first, only one tree burns, but then a whole forest is set ablaze. No matter how hard we try to cover it with polite language, calling it "a helpful critical comment," or "speaking the truth in love," much of our speech directed at believers is carnal and demonic. It is the low form of communion of saints.

It is easy to think we can criticize each other without it having an impact. But the opposite is true. Such criticism, when unchecked through healthy dialog, can provide a pathway for the enemy to land in our camp.

I've heard it said that "marriages are made in heaven, but they come in little kits which we must assemble on earth." The same could be said of church life. For a church to have a healthy and successful life, the ability of the people to live together is critical.

Although the problem of speaking against each other can show up in all areas of church life, it is perhaps most pronounced in the relationship of the congregation to the church leader. We'll look at some principles of resolving conflict with leaders, principles which easily apply to communicating with others in the church.

When we have criticism of a leader, we need to ask ourselves if this is a complaint we have felt for some time. Most issues resolve themselves with time, and we, as well as the leader, need time for things to change.

We must ask ourselves if what God is saying to us is intended only for building our own character, and not for correcting our leader. A message for us is not necessarily a message for our leader. Our leader may be the instrument God uses to break open an area of need in our lives. So we want to be aware that our disappointment or anger with our leader may have more to do with our own painful issues than with anything the leader is doing wrong.

We must always first speak our concerns to our leader before we men-

tion them to anyone else. This is the most frequently violated rule of church life and a demonic influence in congregational controversy. We mustn't try to find a support group to lobby for our position. If our words for the leader are from God, we will not need a support group. Simply saying what God has placed on our hearts is enough.

Dialog is the best way to share with a leader. Begin humbly, asking questions, probing with a listening ear. Do not begin with accusations and charges. No one responds well in such an environment.

If after dialog we still disagree with the leader, then make the issue a subject of prayer. We can ask God to open our leader's eyes so he can see the truth of what we have said. We must continue to be gracious to our leader, letting him know that our disagreement has not broken our respect and appreciation for him.

Personal Side of Evil

We have been talking about the suprapersonal side of evil, where the devil gives assistance in tearing apart the church. But evil also has a *personal* side. The devil often incites us to do evil in the areas of our own lusts, sins which destroy the church in a different way.

James 4:2-4 describes believers at war with one another. They are praying like nice Christians, but their prayers are only a means of murdering other people. I have actually had people tell me they are praying for my defeat, people who call themselves believers.

If we ask the average Christian if they are a "hedonist," a person controlled by their pleasures, they would say, "Certainly not!" But James says that these conflicts come from religious pleasures *(hedono).*

We like our religious life in a certain way. It must not hurt or be uncomfortable. We do not want to submit to anyone, because we would rather maintain control. Our religion must work to our best interest, making us look good and allowing us to get our way. Whenever people—especially leaders—threaten our religious pleasures, we react by quarreling and fighting. This is especially true when God is putting his finger on an area of sin or need in our lives. Are there certain religious pleasures governing our lives? If there are, James calls this adultery, trying to live with the world and be the bride of Christ at the same time.

Such adultery is the fertile soil for church division. It works like this: Our religious desires, the ways we like our religion, are unseen when things are going our way. Then something happens to threaten one of our cherished religious values, and suddenly we are ready to defend what we perceive as non-negotiable. This religious hedonism gives demonic spirits the opportunity to assist us in fulfilling our desires. Soon we begin to gossip about our feelings and gather a group of like-minded people to fight all those who stand in our way. The party we choose is the party which best responds to our religious pleasures. We are even prepared to divide what Christ has put together (Eph 4:3). No wonder James writes such harsh words to people like this.

> Wash your hands, you sinners, and purify your hearts, you double-minded. Grieve, mourn and wail. Change your laughter to mourning and your joy to gloom. Humble yourselves before the Lord, and he will lift you up. (Jas 4:8-10)

However, there is an encouraging factor, even though the devil is waging a war with which our flesh agrees. Even against two seemingly unbeatable foes, God is coming to aid us in the assault (Jas 4:4-6). When we loiter with the world, God gets jealous. He has put his Spirit in us and wants our spirits to be faithful to his leading. Like a jealous lover, he moves in, pouring out more grace so we will be more taken with him than with our own lust. The destiny and glory of the believer, as the spotless bride of Christ, are not threatened by the assault of the devil nor by the carnality of the Christian. God will not let the enemy overrun the church or disembowel the spirit of the believer. He is fighting on our behalf, giving grace to the humble.

How do we fight when we see the manifestations of our own lust and the presence of the devil? The instructions are quite clear.

Submit to God (4:7). We are to place ourselves back under his authority in a covenant of obedience. We are to let his ambitions and desires govern our lives.

Resist the devil (4:7; 1 Pet 5:9). Resisting the devil is verbal, as we demand evil spirits leave our presence and stop harassing us, but it is probably mostly mental. It demands a toughness of mind that does not allow demonic thoughts to penetrate. It means pushing back the enemy with aggressive thoughts and behavior for the kingdom. We resist by pushing back. We resist by advancing.

Come near to God (4:8). "Come near" is used of the Jewish priest drawing near to God in worship, and likewise we draw near through worship (Lev 10:3; Ex 19:22). Here is where God comes near to us. Worship affirms the victory which is ours in Christ and lifts us up to see events and people from God's perspective. It gives God an opportunity to speak to our own hearts in both correction and affirmation. Here, in worship, we can wash our hands and purify our hearts, and appropriately deal with the sin which is plaguing us.

If we are filled with selfish ambition, envy, bitter quarreling and conflict, our hearts can be opened by God to receive his blessing as we worship him with integrity. The devil cannot interfere in worship of the living God when it is offered in humility and integrity. And this communion with God is our best tool in spiritual warfare.

9 Beware of False Prophets

I N 1938 ORSON WELLES SHOCKED AMERICA WITH HIS RADIO dramatization of an outer-space invasion. Although several announcements were made during the broadcast of "War of the Worlds" citing its fictional nature, thousands of people were panicked by the presentation. They were simply not able to discern fiction from fact.

Likewise, Satan plays on our lack of discrimination and would love to lead us away from God by using false prophetic words. The corruption of this God-given gift should not cause us to shy away from prophecy, but rather to learn to be more cautious and discerning. The gift of prophecy is so desperately needed in the church that it will be worth our time and trials to learn to discriminate between true and false prophecy.

False prophecy in the church should not surprise us. It is an element of the last days. But so is the increased power of the Holy Spirit. Scripture teaches that the end of the last days will be characterized by two great revivals: the revival of sin under the unholy trinity of the beast, the false prophet and the antichrist, and the revival of the power of the Holy Spirit through a fuller and final completion of the Joel prophecy (Acts 2:17-21).

How do we know that we are living in the last days? It's common to hear Christians say that these are "the end times," and though that is theologically true, their proclamation is often intended as an eschatological comment on our times. However, this is not exactly how the term is used in the New Testament. "Last days" refers to the period of time between Christ's death and his return to earth (Heb 1:2; 1 Pet 1:20; Acts 2:17). The term "day of the Lord" refers to the events at the end of the "last days" (1 Thess 5:2; 2 Thess 2:2-3; 2 Pet 3:12).

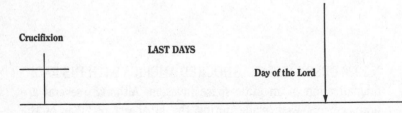

So it is quite proper to say we are living in the last days, although this is not saying anything profound. However, if a friend says, "I think the day of the Lord is near," then we will want to judge his words carefully.

A major characteristic of the revival of sin will be the increased appearances of false prophets. These false messengers will be used to seduce and deceive believers. If the enemy can turn a Christian in a wrong direction through prophecy, we can be sure he will try to do so. Satan tries to counterfeit the genuine gifts from God. Therefore, the best defense against false prophecy is to know the true gift of prophecy and how it is to be exercised. With increasingly hard and chaotic times, people will seek out those who know the future (Mt 12:38-39). They will discount God's revelation and his prophets, and find prophets of their own making. To battle this, we will also need revelatory gifts, which God will supply.

False Prophets Are Coming

One cannot escape the frequent mention of false prophets in New Testament eschatology. They will come claiming to be *the Christ* and through their prophecies they will mislead many (Mt 24:5, 11). In their ministry, they will manifest *great signs and wonders,* so much so they will tempt the elect to fall away (Mt 24:24). Like Jezebel in Thyatira, they will work themselves into church leaderships and will have a significant role model in the false prophet who assists the work of the beast (Rev 2:20; 13:11-18; 19:20). We do not need to look too far to see these people, because they are with us now. New Age and occult activities are producing a herd of false prophets who see the future and grant personal, corporate and national prophecies. Today, people are encouraged to collect around themselves their own cadre of sages and diviners in order to live successful lives.

Principles of Prophecy

Unlocking prophetic gifts within a church is much like opening Pandora's box. It is an invitation to confusion, anxiety, interpersonal conflict and a host of other pastoral problems. Prophecy is like dynamite. Used correctly, it can move mountains. But when used wrongly, it can blow off our hands and hurt others in the process. No wonder Paul gave this advice to the Thessalonians:

> Do not put out the Spirit's fire; do not treat prophecies with contempt. Test everything. Hold on to the good. Avoid every kind of evil. (1 Thess 5:19-22)

There is a carnal tendency in all churches to pour water on the work of the Holy Spirit and thus put out his fire. This carnal pull is always at work, particularly so with the gift of prophecy. It is something which is easy to treat with contempt. We would rather not go through the pains-taking process of sifting prophecy, testing its content. As a lazy church, we would accept prophetic words carte blanche or be rid of them all together, rather than go through the work of discerning the good from the evil. And there is both good and evil in prophecy, and thus the need of discernment.

Nowhere in Scripture does it state that the gifts of the Spirit have ceased. Arguments which suggest Scripture supports this position are usually based on bad exegesis, a deduction from theology, or an argument from silence. All observers of post-apostolic history are aware of the de-cline of certain gifts in the church. Decline, however, is vastly different from withdrawal. As David Aune says, regarding the gift of prophecy: "In early Christianity, as in Judaism, the gradual decline of prophetic activity is attributable to social rather than theological factors."[1] The primary reason these gifts have not reappeared is that we do not want them, or we fear using them.

The outpoured Spirit on the day of Pentecost made the prophetic potential of every believer a reality (Jer 31:31-34; Acts 2:17-18). "Proph-ecy," says Gerhard Friedrich, "is not restricted to a few men and women in primitive Christianity. . . . It is a specific mark of the age of fulfillment that the Spirit does not only lay hold of individuals but that all members of the eschatological community without distinction are called to proph-esy."[2] Since Jesus gave himself so completely to us through the Spirit, Paul had no hesitation in encouraging the Corinthians to "eagerly desire spiritual gifts, especially the gift of prophecy" (1 Cor 14:1).

At the same time, it is also true that the New Testament church rec-ognized specific men and women to be prophets. These individuals were often itinerant and ministered alongside residential teachers and pastors. Some, such as Agabus, were noted for their forecasting ability (Acts 11:27-30; 21:10-14). Others like Judas, Silas and the daughters of Philip "encouraged and strengthened" the churches with lengthy messages (Acts 15:32). There were also residential prophets among the elders akin to those at Lystra who laid hands on Timothy and spoke God's appropriate word (1 Tim 1:18; 4:14).

Prophecy today, although it may be very helpful and on occasion overwhelmingly specific, is not in the category of the revelation given to us in Holy Scripture. "All Scripture is God-breathed" (2 Tim 3:16). I take this to mean Scripture is God's exhalation, his breathing out of his Word. That Word was given to the prophets and apostles by the Holy Spirit and was written down. These writers were "carried along by the Holy Spirit" (2 Pet 1:20-21) to accurately communicate the will of God to his people. This was no automatic writing, for each of the authors retained his own style, but each was surrounded by the Holy Spirit to such an extent that their writings were free of personality-induced flaws and theological error. Therefore, to believe in "verbal inspiration" means we believe each and every single word of Scripture is inspired of God; hence, Bible words are important. "Plenary inspiration" means that the whole of Scripture, its themes and systems, is inspired and without error.

Because of the special category of Scripture as God-breathed or inspired, it is inappropriate to treat modern-day prophecy in the same way. The Bible uses the term *revelation (apocalupsis)* to refer to prophetic ministry (1 Cor 14:26, 30). This revelation must be harmonious with the inspired writings of the prophets and apostles for it to be approved (1 Cor 14:37-38).

Revelation can be divided into three categories. *General revelation* is the revelation which comes through creation, to all mankind, manifesting God's existence (Rom 1:20). *Special revelation* is the revelation which comes through Scripture, illuminated by the Holy Spirit, proclaiming God's existence and his salvation to all who believe. This word is absolute and binding upon every person, in all cultures, throughout all generations. *Specific revelation* is the revelation of the Holy Spirit which gives specific guidance and encouragement to specific individuals, in specific places, at specific times.

In *general revelation,* God reveals himself in creation (Gen 1). In *special revelation,* God gives his Word through chosen instruments, apostles and prophets, who are supernaturally aided (inspired) to deliver God's Word in verbal and written forms. In *specific revelation,* a believer is given a word by the Holy Spirit for themselves or someone else. This revelation may be verbal, in which the speaker knows God's exact words for the person, or plenary, in which the speaker knows the theme God is weaving for the person.

As accurate as prophetic words may be today, Scripture maintains that they are only "in part" (1 Cor 13:9). Thus, prophetic words are only specific revelation and not special revelation, and must be judged (1 Cor 14:29). Such judgment is not necessary for Scripture, since it is already approved by God.

There will be times in which a person will prophesy with 100 per cent accuracy. The words will be verbally revealed, the whole content will be God's concern, and the tone will reflect God's character. The person for whom the word is given receives the message. This prophetic word will necessitate little discernment.

On other occasions, the prophet will speak with only 75 per cent accuracy. (Forgive the mechanical percentage, but I think it makes the point.) The prophet may hear the words from God, and know the intention of God's heart, but fail to communicate the tone of God. They may substitute their own tenor, thus giving a shape to the message which God did not intend. This prophecy is still prophecy, although it is not absolutely pure, and will demand a small correction by discernment. This should not disturb us because we realize we are not "inspired" and will occasionally substitute, unwittingly, our own interpretation of God's revelation. We are learners together, and this is no great sin. Unless a specific contradiction to Scripture occurs, we need to be forgiving and learn together.

Testing Prophecy and False Prophets

The gift of prophecy is incredibly valuable to the church, but all believers, especially elders and pastors, need to be on their guard for those who would sneak into the fellowship to deceive the elect (Mt 7:15). Scripture gives the following guidelines for the use of this gift. First, we will look at guidelines for spotting false prophets (from the Old Testament), and then we will look at guidelines for the use of prophecy (from the New Testament).

Old Testament Guidelines. The Old Testament gives three specific ground rules for spotting a false or true prophet. *First, if a prophet invites us to go off and worship another god, whether creature or spirit, that person is a false prophet and is to be put to death* (Deut 13:1-5).

Second, if the prophet speaks a word, claiming it to be from the Lord, but later it is discovered that the word did not originate with God, that prophet is to die (Deut 18:20).

Third, the false prophet will be spotted if what he speaks does not come true, for what God says will always be fulfilled (Deut 18:22).

Probably we have heard the definition of a prophet as one who foretells and forthtells. A wider definition, as formulated by Wayne Grudem, has these component parts.[3] An Old Testament prophet was a "messenger from God, sent to speak to men and women with words from God" (Hag 1:13). Such prophets claimed "their very words were words which God had given them to deliver" (Ex 4:12; Ezek 2:7). God is therefore referred to as the speaker of the prophet's words. To disbelieve or disobey a prophet's words was to disbelieve or disobey God, for the words of the true prophet were beyond challenge or question (1 Sam 3:19). There was no sifting or evaluation to be done. Last, the Old Testament prophet was God's exclusive spokesman for authoritative revelation. That is why the standards for Old Testament prophecy were so important.

New Testament Guidelines. A question that is frequently asked about prophecy is: "If in the Old Testament they stoned a prophet for a false message, why do we not have the same high standard in the New Testament and in the church today?" Grudem's answer to this question is most helpful.[4] In the Old Testament the *authoritative* revelation of God came through his prophets. Therefore, if they were in error, they were false prophets. In the New Testament, that high standard of revelation rests on the apostle, not the prophet. It is only the apostles who speak with authoritative revelation from God. Therefore, latitude is given to New Testament prophecies which was not given in the Old, because the words they spoke were not thought to be God's very words (Eph 2:20).

There are a few reasons why we know this was true. As with the words of Old Testament prophets, apostolic words in the New Testament were binding and not to be challenged or evaluated (1 Cor 14:37-38). New Testament prophecy, however, is to be evaluated and sifted, sorting the good from the bad; hence, it is not to be thought of as God's very words (1 Cor 14:29; 1 Thess 5:19-21). No prophetic word could ever overturn an apostolic word (1 Cor 14:36-38). Occasionally, the apostles disobeyed a prophetic word (Acts 21:4-5), and some New Testament prophecies seem to have small mistakes (Acts 21:10-11, 32-33; 22:29).

There are also guidelines given regarding the practice of prophecy as well as the character of the prophet. *Uncontrolled frenzy in a prophet does not testify to the Spirit of God.* The true gift of prophecy manifests itself by a quiet spirit which is subject to the will of the prophet (1 Cor 14:32). Prophecy itself was nothing new in the Greco-Roman world, of which Corinth was a part. Prophetic arts were an integral feature of all social and religious life. David Aune reports that "knowledge of the future was indispensable for reducing the risks inherent in a great variety of human activities."[5] What marks the *true* gift of prophecy is a quiet spirit which is subject to the volition of the prophet (1 Cor 14:32).

Paul's words on prophecy are helpful to us today as well. The mantic arts of the Greco-Roman world had characteristics which are still seen today, but foreign to New Testament prophecy. The communicator of the oracle went into a state of divine possession, much like a modern "channeler." A spirit would descend upon the person, overtaking control of his body. The oracle would often go into a manic frenzy; it was believed that the crazier the "prophet" got, the more authentic was their word. Drugs were also used to induce prophetic experiences. Prophets normally took the initiative to call spirit guides by using magic, obeisance and incantations. This ungodly prophecy was also marked by a lack of moral or religious content. The communiques dealt strictly with the future and decisions to be made.

Only two or three prophecies are to be given at any one meeting (1 Cor 14:29). This prophetic guideline is given for the benefit of the listeners. More than three prophecies given at once can glut our understanding and can make us dull to the Word of God. I would here distinguish between prophecies which are for the whole church, of which there are to be up to three, versus personal prophecies, of which there can be as many as needed (1 Tim 1:18; 4:14).

Each prophecy is to be judged (1 Cor 14:29). Aune summarizes the judgment in the following way: The evaluation process was not formal, nor was it executed with a negative attitude. There was no noticeable pause in the meeting while the word was being critiqued. Since believers had the Spirit and could hear from the Spirit, the responsibility of the evaluation belonged to the congregation. Certainly other prophets and elders in the assembly gave leadership to the evaluation process. In this evaluation, the content of the prophecy was important (2 Thess 2:1-3; Gal 1:8-9).[6]

Listed right alongside prophecy in Paul's listing of spiritual gifts is the gift of "distinguishing between spirits" (1 Cor 12:10). Distinguishing between spirits finds its root in the word for *judging* (1 Cor 14:29). This may mean that distinguishing between spirits was a complementary gift to prophecy, just as interpretation is to glossolalia.

Prophetic words are to be measured by the revelation of the Old and New Testaments (2 Tim 3:16-17; 1 Cor 14:37-38). True prophecy submits gladly to the final authority of Scripture, for it is not new revelational truth for the church, but a harmonic expression of that truth.

Prophetic speech must meet certain theological criteria. The apostle John offers a test for true prophecy in 1 John 4:1-3: a true prophet will acknowledge that Jesus has come in the flesh. This is but one measure of a prophet's Christology. If a prophet cannot acknowledge Jesus, then this prophet is not from God.

Prophetic speech should flow out of the character of Jesus Christ, *because the "testimony of Jesus is the spirit of prophecy"* (Rev 19:10; Jn 14:26). As James Dunn has said, "If the Spirit is by definition the Spirit of Jesus, then Jesus himself becomes the basic criterion by which we know the Spirit."[7]

Jesus told us we would know false prophets, and hence false prophecies, by their character (Mt 7:15-20). Bruce Yocum emphasizes this point:

When we examine the statements of the New Testament and the early church manuals in regard to discerning prophecy, we are first of all struck by the fact that they are almost exclusively concerned with discerning prophets rather than prophecies. The warnings of the epistles are directed towards false prophets, not specific false prophecies. Similarly, the *Didache* gives rules for determining whether a prophet is true or false, not whether his prophecies are true or false. (11:5, 6, 12)[8]

The postapostolic church fathers were thoughtful on this subject and gave additional guidelines for prophetic protocol. There should be no private readings where the prophet takes a person off in a corner, because this removes them both from the judgment of the whole church. The normal and safest context for the exercise of the gift of prophecy is in the worship service (1 Cor 14:26). Certainly there will be private words for individuals, but it is still safest to give these in the presence of two or three witnesses. Further, no money is to exchange hands, for the prophet should not charge for his services. Paying prophets is dangerous business, and any income they receive should be separate from the ministry, or at least anonymously given. Last, the prophet was not to respond to inquiries by people, but only to speak when God spoke to him.

Why Do We Need Prophetic Words?

Why do we value the gift of prophecy? *People are personally strengthened by this gift* (1 Cor 14:3; 1 Tim 1:18). I shall never forget the first time I was prophesied over by someone who had a strong prophetic anointing. Eighteen months before, I had been taken to the hospital for an apparent heart attack. Since that day, I had worried about the condition of my heart and the length of my life. The prophet regarded me silently for a moment as I sat with four of my closest friends and half a dozen onlookers. Finally he spoke: "You think you're going to die of a heart attack, don't you? The Lord wants you to know you are not going to die of a heart attack." All of my friends began to laugh because they knew the fear which had gripped me. That simple word, which assured me that God knew my situation (and cared enough to reveal it to the prophet), left me with great comfort and took away my fear of dying by heart attack.

Spiritual gifts are released through the gift of prophecy (1 Tim 4:14). Paul establishes the principle of elders laying on their hands, speaking words of prophecy and releasing spiritual gifts.

One evening, I gathered all my leaders together for a time of prayer and gift release. Another pastor joined me, and together we prayed over most of the people in the group. As Bob prayed for one particular woman, he began to sing over her in a spontaneous, spiritual song. Bob asked the woman if she was a singer. "Not a church soloist or anything," she replied. Bob went on, "But, God does give you songs at home, and you sing them, don't you?" "Why, yes!" she said. Bob asked if God had given her a song that day. She said he had, so Bob instructed her to sing it for the entire group. From that moment on, the woman was released in the gift of spontaneous songs, and she would sing whatever the Lord placed on her heart. Like that woman, most of us need prophetic prayer for spiritual gifts to be released in us.

Life direction may be revealed prophetically (Acts 13:1-3). I have seen people receive direction for life changes such as new jobs through prophetic words. One family in our church came to talk to us about a prophetic word they had received. They believed they were to leave their present location and come to be with us. Shan and DeeAnne had asked God to confirm his word to them *five times* so that they would be sure that they were moving in the right direction. Telling no one, they waited and prayed. The words of confirmation began to come in almost immediately. Over the course of two weeks, they heard over and over again that they were to move. The last confirmation came from a friend who simply said, "I don't know what this means, but the Lord told me to tell you that I am the fifth." Shan and DeeAnne needed no more assurance.

Relationships may be healed by this gift (Acts 15:28, 32). A prophet once told me why I was having conflict with another brother. It seems I had withheld a material object from a friend. The prophet had seen the object in a dream, and said this was the source of our conflict. I immediately made restitution, and our relationship was restored.

Guidance is given and the future will be revealed (Acts 16:6-10; 11:27-28; 20:23; 21:10-11). Another prophet told a man in my church, in a public meeting, that he was about to come into a large amount of money. I told the man that if this was to be the case, he needed to learn now how to manage the money God was about to give him. I then sent another man over to give him some counsel on biblical stewardship. The man followed the advice in a detailed way. Within a week, a mining stock he owned doubled in price and split two for one, giving him a large amount of money.

Sins will be revealed by this gift (1 Cor 14:24-25). God still reveals the sins of people, and when the gift of prophecy is used with pastoral wisdom and love, this can be of great benefit to the body. One of my friends was praying for a stranger to our church. As my friend prayed, he saw by the Spirit a street corner, an elementary school, a pornographic theater and the man entering the theater. When he described what he saw and asked the man if he had ever been to the theater, the man broke in repentance, confessing a weekly habit. I have seen this same thing happen many, many times. By prophetic word, God reveals people, places and events that are sinful and need correction.

These six areas of prophetic ministry are absolutely essential in the church today, and certainly necessary if we are to do battle with the enemy. But we must keep in mind that prophetic words are at the Lord's disposition, not the prophet's. Our focus must be upon God, not on some search for prophetic words. God will release words for us when they are required.

Who Do We Listen To?

Those who prophesy have different levels of anointing; some are more mature and hear with greater accuracy, and others are less experienced and may be more prone to error. However, every word which is given by a caring Christian should be received with appreciation. We want to encourage those who are developing this gift. At the same time, we are to humbly weigh and judge every word spoken. The person giving the word is not the one to determine the accuracy of it. No one else can bear that responsibility for us.

Because it is so difficult to receive accurate prophecy for or about someone we are emotionally involved with, we will want to have caution in giving and receiving such prophecies. We will also want to be aware that sometimes a prophet's strong personal opinion can affect his word if he is not careful. If we are given a word that just doesn't sound like it is what the Lord has for us—particularly if it is a strong rebuke—we might say something like this: "I want to keep my heart open before the Lord to hear from him at anytime. However, I don't think this is his word to me, so I must reject it."

As we have said, prophets, even if they function at the highest level of anointing, are not giving authoritative revelation as in Scripture. It would be a grave mistake to let our reverence for a prophet elevate his word above the Lord's. My friend Bob had to face this dilemma once. He was told by a group of pastors that the Lord was leading him to go to Egypt. But as Bob listened to the Lord, he did not feel that God was directing him this way. Bob took the heat from those pastors when he did not go, but he believed he was honestly seeking God's guidance, and

God's answer had been *no.*

The most trustworthy prophet is the one who is quick to hear and slow to speak (Jas 1:19), and the one who functions under pastoral covering. We want to hear from people who listen to the Spirit rather than read personalities. And when someone gives us a prophetic word, it needs to be confirmed by two or three witnesses. Has the Lord confirmed the word in our heart? Have we received similar words from other people? If we took this word before the church, would they agree with our response to it? Last, words from a true prophet always produce conviction, not condemnation. If we feel condemnation, it is most likely not God speaking.

Understanding Prophetic Words

In every situation, God requires that we seek his face in a dedicated and disciplined way. Prophets are no substitute for personally seeking God. In fact, prophets are occasionally released in our midst to test the sincerity of our hearts toward God (Deut 13:1-3). We must realize that some situations will be resolved by wisdom, while others will need prophetic revelation. Revelation is not necessarily superior to godly wisdom, nor is the cognitive process superior to the intuitive. Only when the Spirit is not informing and conforming the mind is it to be viewed as inferior. Prophecy is something God fulfills according to his Word, not something we fulfill according to our efforts. At the same time, we are called to exercise faith and obedience in our walk, as well as persistent prayer that the promises of God be manifested in our lives.

One of the great mistakes in prophecy is to hear it correctly, but to wrongly interpret what has been said. Unfortunately, it is very easy to hear only what we want to hear, even with prophecy. The first interpretation of a prophecy may not be the true one. Prophets may see an event correctly, but not know when the event will take place. Sometimes a prophetic word will be given as one event, when in fact a series of events will fulfill the word. And there are occasions when a prophetic word will be wrong, and we will be hurt in the process. This is particularly true with words about romance, marriage and babies.

Although it can be disheartening when we receive incorrect prophetic words, there are a few ways to prepare for that. First off, we want to begin by being as discerning as possible when the prophecy is given. Paul reminds us in his letter to the Corinthians that prophets only speak "in part," so we must understand their prophecies in that context (1 Cor 13:9). We must forgive the mistaken prophet, and acknowledge that we were not as discerning as we could have been. We also need to make sure that no bitterness toward God rests in our own heart, so that we don't hinder ourselves from hearing true words that God would speak.

Prophecy is usually not literal, but takes decoding to know the meaning.[9] For this reason, it's a good idea to tape record or have someone write down what is said so that we can go over it from time to time. To interpret a prophecy, we must realize that it may be given in prophetic language. For example, "suddenly" or "immediately" may mean fifty days, or the end of the age. "Now" or "this day" may mean as long as thirty-eight years. The promise of patience may mean tribulation is coming to produce the patience. The promise of wisdom may mean God will allow some problems and situations to arise which are beyond our capacity to solve. The promise of a great victory may mean we will enter a great battle, if we are not already in one. The promise of success may mean a series of humbling experiences which set the stage for success in God's eyes. Prophetic words need careful interpretation.

False Prophets, Bad Prophecies

In the secular world, manifestations of power and accurate predictions of the future are the sole criteria for prophecy. This is not so in the church. In order to discern the true gift of prophecy, we need to reveal the counterfeit spirits which attack the church through false prophecy.

Message: An examination of true prophecy begins with an analysis of the prophet's understanding of Jesus Christ. A corrupt Christology, or doctrine of Christ, will produce heretical theology and practice. What do the prophets say about Jesus Christ? Do they confess he is truly God and truly man? Was he eternally with the Father, "begotten and not made"? And when he was on earth, was he fully human? Was he truly tempted in all things like us, yet without sin? And was he the only man who could make propitiation for our sins, pleasing the Father's just wrath? Orthodox answers to these questions will keep us from listening to strange voices.

Character: Does the prophet live in purity, simplicity and transparency (Mt 7:15-20)? Do we have access into his or her private life, knowing what happens behind closed doors? If we do not know them personally, do we have reliable references on their credibility (1 Cor 16:3)? Samuel openly invited an examination of his character (1 Sam 12:1-5), and any true prophet of God will do the same. Closure and hiddenness can spell cover-up of a false prophet.

Personality: Many who prophesy are entirely orthodox in their theology and ethical in their morality, yet are suffering emotionally. They sound like they have a word from the Lord, but the revelation is filtered through soulish baggage. They are angry, not because God is angry, but because they are emotionally unhealthy. They speak with condemnation, not because God condemns, but because they live under the law and have never discovered the grace of God. Their pathology is their theology. Such lack of emotional health is not a good place to find the word of the Lord. Confusion on this matter will cause many to trust spurious words.

Infiltration: Many churches, as they first explore the reality of the Spirit's gifting, will be easily misled by false words. A home Bible study began to listen to the Lord and pray for its members. A stranger joined the group and immediately had "prophetic words" for various members. At first, the group was thrilled because of the aptness of the revelation. As time went by, however, people began to be suspicious; they felt a "check" in their spirits. The Bible study leader decided to investigate and found that the newcomer had been trained in New Age philosophy. The "prophet" saw nothing wrong with his training, and was vague in his discernment between the voice of God and other voices. The study leader then made the difficult decision to ask this newcomer not to return to the Bible study.

Given the saturation of New Age teaching, all of us will run into professing Christians who have been deceived by the philosophies of men, and whose false prophesying may endanger our flocks. Our response to these folks should be to first help them rectify their thinking. If they can be rescued through repentance and correct teaching, then we should help. However, if for the time being they are deceived and unwilling to leave their spirit guides, we should have no more contact with them (Tit 3:10).

We can also anticipate infiltration from occult and Satanic groups, whose intention is to bring about confusion and division. They are like political moles, waiting for their time of prominence. Many are deceived because these "prophets" know all the right language. However, proper vocabulary and manners are not sufficient guides. We must know how to recognize true believers by more than how they talk and act. As soon as a mole is discovered, we must present the gospel to them and give them the opportunity to know the true God. Their refusal to accept the gospel must mean their dismissal, no matter how deep our relational ties with them.

Naiveté: Three things make us vulnerable to false prophecy. The *pack mentality* can affect all of us at times. If the group thinks it's okay, we discard any personal reservations we may have and opt to go along with the crowd. We are also vulnerable to *personality cults* and find it hard to disagree with anyone who knows more than we, or who is hailed as an authority. Thirdly, we can overzealously embrace all of the prophecies we hear. This *lack of discernment* can lead us to accept false prophecies along with true ones in our fear of missing God's voice.

Our resources for avoiding false prophecy are rich. The apostle John's words give us reason to believe that Christians have more discernment in perceiving false prophets than false prophets have in fooling us. He also argues that believers have the supreme duty of private judgment, by the Spirit, in prophetic matters (1 Jn 2:20; 4:1-4). John's confidence in the sufficiency of the Holy Spirit as our guide should keep us from unnecessary condemnation.

10 Contending with Superspirituality

THE LITTLE ENGLISH WOMAN SHOOK HER FINGER AT ME, shouted in what she would have called "tongues," and rebuked me for my behavior. I had told a friend of hers that, according to my understanding of Scripture, her friend was not qualified to give a prophetic word in our church. My accuser was as mad as a hornet and suggested I was "halting the work of God," among other transgressions. This drama went on in full view of the Sunday-morning congregation. Unfortunately, this was not a one-time disruption. The woman went on to sow division in our church: she slandered all the staff, and even went so far as to physically push a staff wife. To top it off, she prayed for my removal as pastor. This woman continued to speak evil of our church long after she had left, until she choked to death on a piece of meat lodged in her throat. This severe illustration reflects a form of spiritual warfare which has caused havoc in the last twenty-five years, especially in and through the charismatic movement.

What were we contending with in this woman? Some would say she was emotionally sick and in need of counseling. Others would say she was an agent of the devil, sent to destroy our work. Still others would say she was trying to control the church. I would agree with all three, and add a fourth. I would say this woman manifested a particular spirit, a spirit which has haunted the church since the first century. Some know this as *superspirituality*; others call it a *Jezebel spirit.* The early church knew something similar, although not identical, and called it *Gnosticism.* Satan's intention in this form of warfare is to blind people to their spiritual needs, and to promote an elitist attitude which polarizes disciples and ultimately divides the church.

Gnosticism

What is Gnosticism? *Gnosticism* comes from the Greek word *gnosis,* which means knowledge. An *agnostic* is one who is uninitiated to knowledge. Until modern times, the term *Gnosticism* was applied exclusively to heretical teachings which were denounced by the apostles and church fathers. Early Gnostics believed that the created world was evil. The spirit world was separate from, in opposition to, and was always to be preferred above the created world. Only those who possessed the "divine spark" could escape the evil creation. Awareness of the divine spark came through enlightenment *(gnosis),* and enlightenment came only to those who were initiated.

New Testament Gnostics

No doubt, some of Paul's problems mentioned in 1 Corinthians were caused by gnostic attitudes. The Corinthians felt they had special knowledge and were therefore exempt from the guidelines of normal believers. Esoteric knowledge may have fueled divisions and spawned their choices in leaders. Although they thought themselves spiritual, they were fighting one another and taking each other to court. They participated in every kind of indulgence, and justified sexual abstinence in marriage. They claimed the temptations of the world were too strong to resist and made a mockery of the Lord's Table by their improper behavior. They emphasized the more dramatic and ecstatic gift of tongues and had to be corrected by the instruction of love. They even denied the bodily resurrection of Jesus and the future resurrection of believers. These Corinthians were very much affected by incipient Gnosticism.

They were not the only early Christians to overemphasize the spirit. Paul had to confront incipient Gnosticism also among the Colossians, who were involved in strange self-abasement practices and depended upon mystical revelations (Col 2:16-23). Ephesus seems also to have been a hotbed for early Gnostic tendencies for at least four decades, which is evident from Paul's warnings to Timothy (1 Tim 6:20-21). Some thirty years later, John was still dealing with the same problem in Ephesus, or at least in the surrounding region. This time they were denying that Jesus appeared in the flesh (1 Jn 4:2-3). Heretics were teaching that Jesus only "seemed" to be in the flesh and in reality was only spirit. This verse came to form a test for Christological orthodoxy (and was not primarily a means of determining demonization).

The Modern Pathology: Superspirituality

Technically, the incipient Gnosticism responded to in the New Testament is not what we are observing in the church today. There, it was a theological problem of Christology which affected the early Christians' behavior. *Today's gnosticism is more emotional; it denies painful realities and avoids correct behavior by a wash of spiritual language.* Though this modern-day phenomenon has an emotional base, demonic spirits can also empower this behavior. The problem becomes two-pronged, so it is best to speak of it as a spirit/behavior conflict.

Where is this problem found today? The typical person with this spirit/behavior has numerous personal and family conflicts, tensions which they cannot see. At the same time these chronic problems fester, the person seems to have a continual stream of "words" from the Lord for the church. These people can paint beautiful religious pictures when their own lives are in ruin.

Bob used to faithfully attend our breaking-of-bread service every Sunday night. Since the service had no formal leader, and anyone was free to speak at anytime, it was always expected that Bob would have a verse to share. Yet Bob's poor relationship with his wife prevented her from even joining him at the service. Bob also had a terrible relationship with his children. Even his employer, the school board, wanted to dismiss him because of his poor performance as a teacher. Yet week after week, Bob would wax on with the new truths he had learned from the Lord. But sadly, the fruit of the Spirit was missing from his life.

Another example is the person who believes they have a word from the Lord, and although they have no pastoral relationship with the church, believe they are to speak the following Sunday morning. The tenor of their words is usually condemning. This spirit/behavior can also be seen in the unmarried couple who sleeps together, but who are convinced the Lord knows their situation and is not upset.

I saw this behavior of superspirituality in the woman who came into my office, found my personal diary and began to read it. When confronted, she was sure "in her spirit" that she had not done anything wrong. Later, she repented and saw her error.

The Superspiritual Mindset

Anyone who counsels such an individual must be aware of the underlying assumptions compelling their actions. We will examine their thinking patterns first and then look at the biblical principles that we need to rest on in confronting them. Last we will talk about some ways of approaching and discipling someone caught in the superspirituality mindset.

My intention as a pastor is not to run these "strange" believers out of the church (for they are not like the gnostics of John's epistles), but rather to train them to fight the enemy at the level of their spirit/behavior attack.

It is therefore helpful to remember what they believe. *The superspiritual believe their spirit is always pure and on target.* They are never wrong in their spirit. There is an absolute certainty in their self-knowledge.

What they think and what God thinks are the same. Their pathology is their theology.

There is no authority greater than their spirit, therefore our comments from Scripture are subject to their spirit. Authoritative revelation is in their spirit, not the Scriptures.

Since their flesh is evil and of little use, there is no reason trying to improve it. The flesh is uncontrollable, with a will of its own, and therefore it can do whatever it wants.

Life is exclusively lived in the spirit realm, hence there is little or no use for the material realm. There is no good reason for a civil tongue, time for smelling the flowers, telling a wholesome joke, or holding our mate close at night.

They know something we do not know, and they believe we will never attain it in our present condition. They have an elitist attitude regarding spiritual knowledge.

Last, they believe their first instinct about a person is always correct; therefore, they have trouble perceiving anyone differently from the way he or she was first perceived.

Biblical Response to Superspirituality
Each of these wrong perspectives must be addressed from a biblical framework, if we are to do warfare with superspirituality. *The fall of mankind was a total fall* (Gen 3:1-24). Every aspect of our lives was impacted by sin (Rom 3:9-23). Thus, all human spirits have the potential for sin and are subject to God's examination (Prov 16:2; Jer 17:9-10). Therefore, no one can claim consistent and absolute certainty about their self-knowledge.

Our spirits must always be subject to the Spirit of God (1 Cor 2:10-16; 14:32). Therefore, all our feelings and intuitions must be examined by the Spirit of God to determine whether they are valid or not.

We are called by Scripture to glorify God with our bodies (1 Cor 6:19-20; Rom 12:1). Therefore, the actions of our bodies are subject to God's observation and judgment. They must be managed in purity.

Everything created by God is good and is to be received with gratitude, being sanctified by the Word of God and prayer (1 Tim 4:4-5; Gen 1). Therefore, God's created world is good and is to be received gratefully.

On the basis of our identification with Christ's death and the indwelling power of the Holy Spirit, we are expected to make progress over the residue of sin still within us (Gen 4:7; Rom 6:12; 8:13; Col 3:5-17). Although we are assured of eventual victory over sin, we must still wrestle with it in the here and now.

Every born-again child of God already has the initiation of God, the indwelling of the Holy Spirit (Rom 8:9; 1 Cor 12:13; Eph 1:13-14; 1 Jn 2:20). Therefore, no believer is above another believer in initiation into God's knowledge. At the same time, each believer needs to pursue new levels of revelation of God's love and power (Eph 1:17).

Judgment is reserved for God, not any human person (Mt 7:1-5; 1 Cor 4:3-5). Therefore, judging one another's spirituality is pointless.

How to Counsel the Superspiritual

How can we help a person living with the enemy's deception of superspirituality? First, we must remember it is a problem involving both spirit and behavior. Since chapter six offers a discussion about spirits (demons), we will now turn to the emotional/behavioral side of the issue.

How do we respond to someone who is constantly superspiritual? Instead of rejecting them, which is exactly what they expect us to do, we need to disciple them. This may take place in personal counseling or in groups. Our goal is to lead them out of deception and into wholeness.

Fears about counseling or joining a discipleship program are fairly common. However, the fears of superspiritual people run to the very core of their being. Unlike those who have lived unreflective lives and suffered the consequences, superspiritual Christians pride themselves on their keen sense of self-knowledge. For many years they have received guidance through their own internal navigational system. Although they may be divorced, have children in prison, and be in financial chaos—regardless of their track record—they still believe their system is the best for them, and that it has proven faithful in the past. Therefore, their predominate fear is that we are going to tamper with their internal guidance system. For them, losing this inner guidance means losing control of themselves and losing God. Counseling becomes a threat to their faith. Therefore, the counselor could be perceived as the enemy of God and destroyer of their soul.

When these folks seek counseling, two things are going on. First, they are acting in a manner which is inconsistent with their own thinking. Why should they put themselves in a position to lose God and control, particularly at the hands of a person who knows less than they? Second, they are admitting a major defeat in their life by saying they need help. This is something which should not happen if their internal guidance system is operating correctly. This contradiction puts the superspirituals in a terrible bind. Over successive counseling sessions, the vulnerable side may show on one occasion, while on another occasion the absolute certainty of self-knowledge will prevail. They are living in conflict with their problem and their system of thinking.

Before meeting with a superspiritual for a counseling session, it might be helpful to do the following things: First, review the principles of their theological grid. Remember, for them, everything is a God/spirit problem and not a relational/material problem. Ask the Lord to show you what is going on in their life and what he wants to say about it. A way to approach this would be to say: "Jane, I want you to know I can't help you. But God's Spirit can help you, and together we can explore some ways for this to happen. Why don't we pray before we start?"

As we conduct the interview, we need to be listening to see if they appreciate our empathy. At first they may enjoy the attention, but at a moment's notice they can quickly become suspicious that we are manipulating them by silence. Silence to them may mean we are trying to "out-reflect them," and they consider themselves masters at this approach. At the same time, they have never met "spiritual" people who listen, since spiritual people usually talk a lot. They may therefore conclude we are not spiritual.

If we sense they are jumpy (if they have made a negative assessment of us) and may bolt the minute the interview is over, we may try another approach. We may try to diffuse their perception with a counterplay. This approach is to be aggressively spiritual with the person. It helps them see that there is some common ground in our frames of reference. We will want to enter their theological world to minister to them. We need to convince them we know something experientially of spirituality. We meet them spirit to spirit, not reason to reason. We might say, "Before you came today, I was praying for you and I sensed God said . . ." and then go on to tell them what we sensed. Or we might say, "May I share with you what God told me today from his Word?" Do not move hesitantly. Be bold and confident. They need to see we have a word from God and that we operate by hearing his voice. Once they believe we do hear from God, they will feel at ease to receive us and to consider what we say. They will also go back and reflect on whether or not they have heard all God is saying to them. These people respond to words of authority from God. "Do you mind if I share with you something the Holy Spirit has been teaching me?" Or "I sense the Holy Spirit wants me to pray for you right now. Do you mind if I pray for you? When I finish, would you pray for me?" We can let ourselves go when we pray for them, with no fear of being dramatic.

There are a few other things which I have found helpful. I also try to affirm their motives. I believe they are good people with good intentions and they are God's children and he cares for them. Any rebuke I give, or any disagreement I bring to their attention, I attempt to keep in the realm of behavior and not motives. I emphasize the importance of the practical, that true faith will be manifested by deeds (Jas 2:14-26).

The greatest temptation we will face is to tell them they have not really heard from God. Although this is partially true, to tell them this is to strike at the very core of their being and will send them running. When I hear a theological justification for bad behavior, it is good for me to say to myself, "Their spiritual justification is to save them from more pain." I find this gives me a compassion for them, empathy I would not otherwise have. Their superspirituality is a way of avoiding personal failure in time management, parenting, marriage relationships, and so on.

As the person leaves the interview, we might want to suggest they meditate on certain passages before they return. The suggested passages should be those which undercut assumptions of superspirituality and put a human face on the gospel. Remain in a position of calm, compassionate, pastoral authority. Any carnal manifestations of anger, impatience or bullheadedness on our part will only convince them we are indeed uninitiated in spiritual things.

Superspirituality Redeemed
Over the years, I have seen superspiritual Christians serve as elders, lead worship and participate in every area of church life. I must say they are usually the most disruptive people a church can have. *The enemy takes advantage of their personal pain, their unreflective theology, and their relational schisms to produce havoc in the church.* They can divide a church as fast as one can peel a banana. If they are not watched and trained, they will get into all kinds of mischief, for the devil will use them in his front-line troops.

However, these brothers and sisters need to be objects of intense prayer and loving acceptance. I have battled with individuals like this long enough to know some of them are most valuable assets to the kingdom. When they begin to see the positive, material side of Christianity, recognizing that "matter does matter," they become wholesome people. They realize how they treat people and what they do with their bodies matters to God. They begin to see they are both body and spirit, and are called to glorify God with both. Released from their deception, with a heightened appreciation of body and spirit, they are a joy to have around.

11 Eleven O'Clock Demons

THE LAST PLACE IN THE WORLD WE WOULD EXPECT DE-
monic manifestations would be at church on Sunday morning.
In fact, we would be shocked to know how much of our worship
of Jesus Christ is interrupted by these forces. You see, *the devil
and his host purpose to hinder the worship of Jesus Christ. So,*
wherever there is genuine worship, we can expect spiritual warfare.

Our starting point is Matthew 28:16-17: "Then the eleven disciples
went to Galilee, to the mountain where Jesus had told them to go. When
they saw him, they worshiped him; but some doubted."

When did this event take place? Most scholars conclude it was not on
Easter Sunday, when Jesus appeared to the women; nor was it seven days
later when Thomas had his skepticism arrested; nor was it even fourteen
days later, when Jesus fried fish with the disciples and recommissioned

Peter. No, this event took place forty days after Jesus' resurrection, after three appearances to the eleven, and after additional miracles had been done in their presence. Jesus, the living and resurrected Lord, is about to commission his newly trained lieutenants. And we find that some of them are worshiping—*but others are doubting.*

Why were they not all worshiping? They had all had sufficient access to the same experiences of the risen Lord. Although the text is silent, let me make this tentative interpretation. I believe their doubt was due to a demonic assault which distracted them from worship. Their spiritual radar screens had been jammed with demonic static. So they could not perceive what was going on nor respond to it.

I have seen this same phenomenon happen many times on a Sunday morning. God has spoken to people through the Scriptures, and their hearts are full of love and thanksgiving. Then, out of nowhere, a wave of doubt comes over the group. People begin to ask themselves a series of questions: Will God meet my need? Does he still love me? Is he worth trusting with my life? Doubt moves in like a fog, displacing the worship.

Satan's Agenda

Why would demons want to interfere with the worship of Jesus Christ? Very simply, they have a different agenda. *It is their intention that Satan and themselves should be worshiped.* This is quite obvious in the temptation narrative (Mt 4:8-11). Satan wanted Jesus to worship him and was even willing to bribe him to do so. He offered Jesus the kingdoms of this world, an offer he could make with legitimacy. From the earliest account in the garden, to the very end of human history, Satan is pressing to receive worship (Gen 3:1-5). The end-time conflict is summarized by who will get worship: the beast and the dragon, or Jesus Christ (Rev 9:20; 13:4; 13:8; 2 Thess 2:4). Scripture says there is just one bright and morning star who is to receive our worship—Jesus Christ. But as long as Satan is on earth, he will attempt to be the bright and shining light who gets our attention (Is 14:12; Rev 22:16).

Occult movies which portray the worship of Satan often obscure the real desire of the enemy. The devil does not merely want liturgy and symbolic ceremony, he wants total devotion and servitude. He believes he is more beautiful than anyone else, hence his need to be adored and honored. All the things which rightly belong to Jesus Christ, including worship, adoration and devotion, Satan wants for himself.

Notice how Jesus responds to Satan's temptations in Matthew 4:10. *He begins with a word of rebuke: "Away from me!"* This is an example of verbal resistance, commanding that the enemy leave our presence. The believer utters such a bold prayer only in the name of Jesus Christ (Jude 9): "In the name of Jesus Christ, I command every evil spirit to leave now!" For some, such boldness may be emotionally awkward. We may feel like actors defying unseen enemies. However, if we can get past feeling foolish, and see our Lord verbally rebuking the enemy, we can use Jesus' example as a model for our own behavior.

Since the temptation was real, Jesus needed to shore up his mind by the Word of God. Jesus' response to the devil is not a specific passage of Scripture, but a summary of several passages from Deuteronomy. He fends off temptation by declaring the Word of God to himself and to the enemy. The Word of God cleanses our minds of mental pollution leaked to us by the enemy. It is a filter which stops harmful agents from entering the sensitive parts of our spirits. It acts like a spiritual antibody, warding off infectious temptations. If Jesus needed such an agent to defend himself, so will we.

After Jesus rebuked him, the devil left Jesus and angels came to Jesus' assistance. Likewise for us, when we have fought temptation by rebuking the enemy and standing mentally with the Word of God, we can expect angels to attend us, particularly as we seek to worship Jesus. On several occasions, angels have been spotted in our worship service. They have stood as armed guards, securing our sanctuary for unhindered worship.

Disruption of Worship

If Satan and his demons are not receiving worship, we can bet they will interfere with the worship of Jesus Christ. How do they halt worship?

As Pharaoh hindered the Israelites, Satan will hinder us from going to worship (Ex 3:12; 4:23). Pharaoh would not let the children of Israel out of his sight, even when great plagues were coming upon his country. He was stubborn, changing his mind only temporarily with the death of his own child (Ex 12:29-31).

Likewise today, Satan will do anything in his strength to prevent people from going to worship Jesus Christ. He will blind them to the beauty of Jesus so that they see no significance in worshiping him. He will encourage them to sleep in, or tempt them to play golf or trim their lawns, as long as it keeps them busy and away from public worship. Have we not experienced the typical Sunday-morning chaos of trying to take a family to worship? Is it not strange that we have such difficulty in getting our families out the door? Do we have the same problem Monday through Friday? Not at all! The enemy does not want us to worship, and he will do anything he can do to stop us.

If Satan and his host cannot halt us from going to worship, he will attend with us, so he can destroy it. This was Satan's approach at the birth of Jesus (Mt 2:8). Herod told the Magi, "Go find the boy, so I can worship also!" What Herod really wanted to do was to destroy the worship of the baby Jesus. He demonstrated his barbarity when he ordered that all the boys in Bethlehem two years and younger be killed (Mt 2:16-18).

Shortly after Jesus commenced his public ministry, he encountered a demonized man in a synagogue (Lk 4:33). Not all demons hide in the pagan world. Many show up at church week after week, eleven o'clock on the button. Believers' bodies can be the best cover for demons, and it's a place from which they can do their greatest damage. Do we think demons are present in our worship service? Most of us would say *no*. But when Jesus went to church, he found demonized people numbered among the saints. And they are still with us, putting a damper on our worship.

In fact, they have been doing it so long we have come to believe the inferior level of worship we usually experience is the norm.

Besides entering the church through demonized Christians, Satan infiltrates the church through people sent by cults and Satanic groups. They come in order to disrupt the worship of Jesus Christ. On more than one occasion, our church has been visited by witches who wanted their evil presence to confuse our worship. Externally, they appeared to be just one of the crowd, but all the while, they are praying against us. Prophetic words I have been hearing suggest that more churches will be invaded by such carriers of demonic spirits in the nineties. They may even become visible and violent in their protest of our worship.

Satan destroys worship by sending teachers who espouse doctrines taught by demons (1 Tim 4:1). Where does the notion that each of us is a god come from? Who encouraged us to believe that the devil and his demons are not real spirits with personalities? Who promoted the idea there is no hell, or that at the judgment all will be saved? Who suggested that the way to please God was for us to work harder? Who encouraged us to believe that orthodoxy (right doctrine) automatically produces orthopraxy (right living)? Demons, instructing Bible teachers, are the source of these deceptions. "Surely," we may say, "my pastor teaches pure Bible truth." Certainly most evangelical pastors are teaching correct doctrine. Yet I have seen many orthodox pastors, full of demons and sin, teaching against grievous sins they are themselves committing. They preach on adultery, and are guilty of it themselves. They condemn pornography one day and read it the next. They commend charity on Sunday and steal from the poor on Monday. They are bound servants, mouthing only what the devil permits.

Satan disrupts worship by showing up at the communion service (1 Cor 10:21). Corinth was a city of the occult, mixing many varieties of pagan religious practices. There were trade guilds with their secret rituals, which had their sources in demonic influence. If a person wanted to be in a particular trade, he would need to be a member of the guild, and hence participate in occult practices. The city also provided an environment for cult prostitution as a means of religious behavior, and offered a wide assortment of idols and mystery religions. It would have been difficult for the Christians in Corinth who wanted to have commercial and social success to avoid participating in these practices. Thus, Paul was concerned some were actually living worldly lives, then coming to the Lord's Supper. His meaning is clear: "You cannot party with the pagans, thinking their demons have no influence, and then expect to come to the eucharist and have its full benefits."

The same holds true today. The church has members who drink to the gods of sex, money and power on Saturday night, and then take communion on Sunday morning. The church also has its members who pledge themselves to secret societies with demonic rituals, then wish to enjoy the benefits of the new covenant sacrament. We need to repent if the table of the Lord is to be honored.

Demons hate the Lord's Supper because it spells an end to their hold on people. One Sunday I was serving communion when I heard a woman crying at the other end of the rail. My wife was with her when a demon began to choke her, not letting her take the bread or the juice. The woman's face was turning purple when we commanded the spirit to release her so she could receive the evidence of God's grace. Demons hate communion and are doing their best to remove it altogether from church life. Many churches spend no more than fifteen minutes per month remembering the Lord in communion. How did such a central feature of the early church take such a back seat? The enemy is out to destroy worship, especially that which remembers Jesus Christ's work on the cross.

Last, the enemy will attempt to provoke a crisis in our lives, a trauma which causes us to curse God, rather than worship him. Job was a devout and morally upright man. He feared God and stayed away from evil men. In his life there was no tension between his godliness and material blessings. He had great wealth, yet he still sought the face of God. His children were also blessed, and there was no indication that they were spoiled children. They appeared to be living in gratitude for the blessings upon their family (Job 1:1-4).

If we are parents, no doubt we have many fears for our children. We are concerned about who they will marry, the grades they need to secure a future, and worse things, such as someone abusing them sexually, or a life-threatening car accident. What Job feared the most was a wrong attitude in the heart of his children. He feared his children would curse God in their hearts. Because of this concern, it was his habit to cover the sin of his children by performing priestly ministry for them, a proper thing for a father to do in those times (1:5).

Parents know how children can carry sorrows and scars in their hearts, wounds which quietly cause them to curse God. It can be a simple thing like a pet dying, or a more profound event like a geographical move from a favorite neighborhood. Events like these can cause children to blame God. "If God is so powerful, why did he let my kitty die?" Their little hearts can quickly become bitter. Thus, parents need to cover their children in prayer before God. We need to be their priests, offering prayers of mercy, forgiveness and protection.

One day, God called his daily staff meeting, with all his angels reporting. On that day Satan, chief of the fallen angels, appeared in the ranks. This appears to be a time before he was thrown down to the earth (Lk 10:18). There is something in the language which suggests he was not an invited guest, but an intruder. God asks him, "Where have you come from?" The Accuser responds, "I've been roaming throughout the whole earth" (Job 1:6-7).

Satan's ministry is accusation, and he spends his whole time roaming, promoting conspiracies of accusation. It has also been predicted that in the 1990s, many church leaders will be falsely accused of sins and crimes they have never committed. They will be truly innocent, but the enemy will cause people to believe that they are guilty. Like Job, they will have to fight to maintain their innocence.

Job 1:8 has got to be one of the great anomalies of the Bible. God says to Satan, "By the way, have you checked out my servant Job?" He holds Job up as one against whom the accuser cannot lodge a legitimate attack. "Yes," said Satan, "I've seen him. And if you did not prop him up, he would curse you. You have blessed him materially, and put a hedge of protection around him." Essentially the enemy was saying Job did not love God, but loved his gifts. He accused him of enduring solely for the benefits and suggested Job would curse God if everything was not well. Notice the accusation. "God, you do not really know the heart of your own servant." And, "It's only a self-serving motive which keeps Job fearing you." Satan then challenges God to reach out his hand and strike Job (1:11). Satan predicts Job will curse God. Francis Andersen translates this verse provocatively, "I'll be damned if he doesn't curse you to your face!"[1] The next two words, "Very well" (1:12), may be the most discouraging words in the Bible—God giving permission for the enemy to test one of his own children.

Does this scenario happen very often? I do not know for sure, but I don't think Job-like situations, with complete destruction, come often. But occasionally God does accept the enemy's challenge to test us. He lets the enemy loose in our direction to show him what is in our hearts.

In Job's case there is one prohibition. Satan is not allowed to touch him physically. No sooner is the permission granted than the Sabeans kill Job's servants and take away his donkeys and oxen. The devil then uses lightning to kill his sheep and some of his other servants. Next, the Chaldeans carry off his camels and slaughter more of his servants. Finally, a tornado strikes the home at which his sons and daughters were feasting, and they are killed. *But in spite of these tragedies, Satan cannot accomplish his mission: to get Job to curse God.*

At this, Job got up and tore his robe and shaved his head. Then he fell to the ground in *worship* and said: "Naked I came from my mother's womb, and naked I will depart. The LORD gave and the LORD has taken away; may the name of the Lord be praised." In all this, Job did not sin by charging God with wrongdoing. (Job 1:20-22, emphasis mine)

So Satan goes to plan 2. He wants permission to attack Job's body, and God agrees, but says he must spare his life. We are uncertain of the disease Job suffered, but it was a skin disease which brought on boils, bad breath and extreme weight loss. In Job 2:8, we find him in the ash heap, scratching himself with a piece of pottery. The enemy then enrolls Job's wife as a co-conspirator in the assault, to encourage Job to curse God. His reply is courageous: "Shall we accept good from God, and not trouble?" (1:10).

Job was not hardhearted and uncaring. He experienced real grief in these tragedies, manifested in tearing his robe and shaving his head. Yet, his first response was to bow low before God, honoring him as God, without raising questions about his God-ness, nor his goodness. In Job, there is no cursing, nor charging God with wrongdoing. He does curse the day he was born (3:1), and he does question the justice of God (27:1), but he never falls into the trap of blaming God. *Further, God never answers the question of why he permitted Satan to attack.* In chapters 38—41, God simply states that he is God, and that he can do what he wants and he will still be proven good. In the end, Job wishes he never opened his mouth in questioning God's justice (42:3). The Lord finally restores Job's life and blesses him more abundantly than at the first (42:12).

Every biblical and philosophical discussion of Job seems to center on the issue of suffering and God's treatment of Job. These issues are no doubt of major importance. However, we cannot overlook Satan's motive and the manner in which Job saw him defeated. *It was an attempt to have Job curse his Creator, rather than worship him.* The concern of the enemy is also to get us to blame and curse God for crisis events in our lives. God's concern, as it was for Job, is that we would be his worshipers no matter what the external circumstances. In any crisis, we have two options—to blame God or to worship him. There may be cases in which we are completely righteous like Job, and yet find major disasters in our lives. We can begin a search for the cause of our trouble and spend years pondering and praying over the questions of Christian suffering. But it was not answered for Job, and I suspect it will not be answered for us either. *Our only option is to do as Job—grieve and worship.* Anything less plays into the hands of the enemy and discredits the sovereign Lord.

Discernment

Discernment of the enemy's attack on our worship is not a simple matter. Many times, after a Sunday service is over, I realize that through various forms the enemy has stolen part of the worship which was due to Jesus Christ. It can come in obvious ways—the heat in the building fails on a particularly cold morning, or the sound system has a mysterious bug—or in subtle ways which take time and a sensitive spirit to ascertain. But I now know worship is not just a matter of music, prayer and devotion. To worship publicly, we must enter a battlefield, strewn with land mines. To be successful in our venture, we need to defuse these bombs before we can truly take the field.

Some ways we can spiritually clear the air for worship are as follows: Privately, invite the presence of the Holy Spirit to fall upon people and to fill the place of worship. Pray for all those who participate publicly, especially those who lead in music and prayer. Occasionally, I have anointed these people and the platform area with oil, dedicating the entire team and facility to the Lord. In doing so, I command any evil spirits present on the stage or harassing people to leave.

I begin the service with an invocational prayer, focusing upon the assured victory of Jesus Christ. In this, we war against any spirits present in the room or on the congregation, and demand they leave and not disrupt worship. We then lead the congregation in bringing their minds into the captivity of Christ, putting away blame and doubt. We then stop our focus on warfare, and put our full attention on loving Jesus Christ.

With all our strength and energy, we pursue one holy calling: the adoration of Jesus Christ.

The enemy leaves when he is not welcome,
when there is no sin he can cling to,
when he is not honored by too much concern,
when the light of God's truth is proclaimed,
and when the Holy Spirit releases an anointing to worship.

IV War on Leaders

12 Thank You, Jonathan Edwards

JONATHAN EDWARDS WAS A BRILLIANT EARLY EIGHT-eenth-century academician, a graduate of Yale, and eventually the president of what was to become Princeton University. He was also a man of powerful religious conviction. Under his anointed preaching, the Great Awakening began in North America in 1734. As a student and practitioner of revival, Edwards was familiar with all of the antics as well as the genuine fruit of revival. One of his helpful writings, particularly discerning in the area of spiritual warfare, is entitled "The Distinguishing Marks of a Work of the Spirit of God."[1] In his paper, Edwards outlines the strategies of the devil to halt advancement of the kingdom of God.

We will review Edwards's five principles of how the devil likes to halt God's work, and look at how they are revealed in the book of Acts and today as we discuss spiritual warfare on leaders, the subject of part four of this book. We will discover that any revival of godliness and spiritual power will automatically produce a wave of opposition. In Acts 4:1-22, we see Edwards's five principles played out in the early church. The devil was trying his best to halt the fragile Christian movement at its inception, alternating between external persecutions *upon* the church to promoting internal dissension and confusion *within* the church. Edwards summarizes the five tactics this way: (1) Satan rages when God begins a fresh work; (2) during periods of revival, people will be misinformed; (3) some people will take offense that they have not been included; (4) others will be jealous; and (5) still others will be outraged because the revival confirms principles they cannot embrace.

Satan Rages

Satan rages against any fresh work of God. In the account given in Acts 3 and 4, why was Satan so upset? Because a forty-year-old man, who had been crippled from birth, was completely and instantaneously healed by the words of the apostles. This healing added an additional 2,000 men to the church, bumping the total to some 5,000 male believers, not counting women and children. This was not just one healing, one conversion or one church; it was the beginning of a *movement.*

Statistics vary on church sizes, but church growth experts suggest that only five per cent of North American churches have more than 200 adults. More often, the average Protestant church's membership numbers in the high sixties, while Catholic church memberships average in the high thirties. Numerically, these present little threat. However, when a movement such as the one in Acts begins to take shape, with large numbers of people zealous for the love of Jesus Christ, Satan pays attention and begins to focus his rage. Richard Lovelace aptly describes this anger:

> The devil, who is losing ground as the revival progresses, fights back in a number of ways. His main strategies are those of accusation and infiltration. He may attack the subjects of revival directly and inter-

nally with despair and discouragement. . . . He may plant lies, caricatures or stereotypes in the minds of unbelievers or unrevived Christians so that they will reject the work of God and attack its progress. If possible, he will set the leaders of the revival against one another in this way in order to divide and conquer. To create evidence to corroborate accusations, he will overbalance the zeal of converts and cause them to run to extremes. Finally, he will sow tares among the wheat in the form of counterfeit revivals, leading people to confound these with the real work which is in progress and to discredit it.[2]

There is a common testimony among those who have led renewal movements: *The beginning of a fresh work was the commencement of spiritual warfare.* Many suffer illness, physical torture and emotional unhealthiness. Still others lose jobs and family members, or experience untimely accidents. The devil uses any means available to halt the momentum of affection for Jesus Christ.

This was the *why* of Satan's rage. What about the *how?* How did Satan show his rage in the Acts account? *The enemy stirred up an emotional reaction in the religious establishment (4:2).* They were "greatly disturbed" by what was going on. This same term is used in Acts 16:18 when Paul is angered by the demonized slave girl who shouted, "These men are servants of the Most High God." Paul was "so troubled" that he commanded the spirit to come out of the girl. This same emotion was felt by the religious leaders. They wanted Peter and John *out* of the temple as badly as Paul wanted the demon *out* of the girl.

During times of revival, it is typical of religious leaders to be hostile toward the work of God, while at the same time permit evil in people's lives. They have little discernment over what is God and what is carnal. There is more concern for religious respectability and tradition than for seeing people get better.

I have many close friends who have been kicked out of their denominations over the last ten years. Gordon is a good example. He is a sensitive and soft-spoken pastor who was told to leave his church, not because of any moral or ethical failure, but because the congregation was afraid of the freshness which had come into his life. He did not introduce theological heresy, only the conviction that God is truly *present.* Congregations and church leaders will one day give account for shepherds like Gordon whom they have rejected.

The leaders of the new work, Peter and John, were thrown into jail (4:3). The term *seized* probably means that they received rough treatment at the hands of the temple police as they hauled them off to prison.

History bears witness that rough treatment of believers often accompanies the spread of Christianity. The encouragement of Hugh Latimer to Nicholas Ridley, as both men burned at the stake in 1555 for their reformation convictions, is apropos for the church throughout its earthly time: "Be of good comfort, Master Ridley, and play the man. We shall this day light such a candle by God's grace in England as I trust shall never be put out!"

At this very moment, Christian leaders in Africa, Asia and South America, the areas of fastest growth for the church, are in prison for their faith. Here in North America, for the first time since segregation struggles in the South, clergy and laymen are being imprisoned for pro-life activities. Such signs of the times may indicate another wave of the Holy Spirit is about to come upon the earth.

Satan further raged through the religious leaders as they warned and threatened the apostles (4:17-18, 21). Physical force would not work, so the Sanhedrin tried intimidation. Verbal abuse is intended to frighten us, to persuade us that man can do something which God cannot stop. This is not true, but our enemy wants us to believe it. And so men and women who are bringing fresh life to the church are threatened with the loss of jobs, pensions and other benefits of the professional ministry. We must learn to recognize this as the discouraging work of the enemy.

Misinformation
During periods of revival, people may be misinformed. The rulers and

elders did not know what was going on, so they had to ask, "By what power or what name did you do this?" (Acts 4:7).

The assumption of the religious leaders who persecuted Peter and John was that personal power, private piety or knowledge had healed the cripple. This is what they imagined. In the ancient Near East, personal power became operative through the use of incantations and the evoking of names. And so it was not uncommon during revivals to hear the accusation that miracles came from occult powers.

The religious leaders, presupposing that it was not God who healed the man, assumed it was by some evil power. Failing that, they assumed that private piety had healed the crippled man. Underlying this thesis is the notion that God only blesses righteous people with healing—which would have meant that the cripple was religiously superior to the Sanhedrin. Since these religious leaders prided themselves on their knowledge, they assumed that if they didn't know about it first, it couldn't be from God.

But it was none of these that healed the man. *The healing took place through ordinary men—men who had been with Jesus, who were filled with the Holy Spirit, and who prayed in Jesus' name.*

Peter and John were unschooled men (4:13). They had not been trained in formal rabbinical studies, which would have required them to memorize great portions of Scriptures and understand all the subtleties of interpretation. They are described as "ordinary men," a term used for laity versus professionals. But as the great German historian Adolf Harnack understood so well, "The great mission of Christianity was in reality accomplished by means of informal missionaries." It was not professional clergy who led the charge, but people whose bellies were full of God and nothing else.

For nearly a dozen years I ministered in the circles of the "Christian Brethren," or what some call the "Plymouth Brethren." These believers broke away from the Anglican church in the early nineteenth century in reaction to the dominance of the clergy over the laity. Over the years the movement has had many noteworthy leaders and subscribers: J. N. Darby,

A. N. Groves, George Müller, H. A. Ironside, Paul Little, F. F. Bruce, to name a few. During my time with the Brethren, I was impressed with "unschooled and ordinary men" who were called to give teaching leadership in the assembly. These were men who usually had no formal theological education, but were able to handle the Scriptures as well as or better than most pastors of the professional pulpit. Seeing these teachers in action revealed to me the subtle prejudice that had been sown in my mind about the laity. I had believed they were incapable of reading and understanding the Bible with any clarity, let alone organizing and teaching anyone else. But it was from the unschooled laity that Jesus founded the church.

Although the disciples' training was not formal, they were relationally trained by Jesus. "They had been with Jesus" (4:13), and that was sufficient qualification for seeing the man healed. Jesus originally called the Twelve not just to be his apostles or "sent-out-ones" (Mk 3:14), but that "they might be with him." The intimacy they were to experience with Jesus was essential to the missionary opportunity they would have in the future. That association gave them confidence that if they prayed for the sick, the One who sent them would back them up.

The religious leaders were also impressed by the courage of these men (4:13). Their courage came from their relationship with Jesus and also from being "filled with the Holy Spirit" (4:8). Luke uses this term nine times in the books of Luke and Acts. The verb for *filling* is not the same as the adjective *full,* which Luke uses in the term "full of the Spirit" (Acts 6:3, 5, 8; 7:55; 11:24) to refer to the general character of the Spirit. Paul describes the same character as "fruit of the Spirit" (Gal 5:22). But when Luke speaks of the *filling* of the Spirit, there are certain things he has in mind.

The filling of the Holy Spirit is repeatable and comes upon individuals as well as groups. It comes upon the 120 on the day of Pentecost (Acts 2:4), upon Peter as he stands before the religious leaders (4:8), on the believers' prayer meeting (4:31), on Paul at his conversion and healing (9:17) and when he rebukes the Cyprus sorcerer Elymas (13:9). Paul's present tense imperative—"be filled with the Holy Spirit" (Eph 5:18)—means we should repeatedly place ourselves in a position to have the Holy Spirit fill us. We need the posture of D. L. Moody who said, "I believe in being filled with the Holy Spirit, but I also believe you can leak."

When they were filled with the Spirit, they were powerfully enabled to minister. The disciples prophesied, spoke in tongues, witnessed, pronounced judgments and healed the sick. Such an incredible encounter with the Spirit does not mesh well with our domesticated North American response to the Spirit. In some traditions, our response to the Spirit is exclusively cognitive. When we are asked to respond to the offer of the Spirit's filling, little seems to happen beyond a mental assent. In other traditions, we seem to focus on the one particular manifestation of tongues. In both traditions, being filled with the Holy Spirit has not translated into active missions work.

So we have a picture of movers and shakers, apostles who were unschooled, ordinary men, who had been with Jesus, who had been filled with the Holy Spirit and so had courage to proclaim the gospel, and who also spoke and prayed in the name of Jesus (Acts 4:10, 12). Because the authority of the apostles was outside of the understanding of the religious leaders of the day, the uninformed Sanhedrin opposed the work of God.

When the renewing presence of God is transforming the church, there will be individuals who are not rightly informed and therefore critical of what is going on. They tend to be trained religious leaders who have not been filled with the Spirit, who spend little intimate time with Jesus, and who have seldom if ever prayed in Jesus' name, particularly for someone to be healed. Since they are not informed on these issues, they will make up stories to explain what is happening according to their theology. As baseball hall-of-famer Dizzy Dean used to say, we need "to call 'em as we see 'em." We need to recognize this opposition to God's work from religious leaders.

Personal Offense

People are offended because they have not personally experienced this work. F. F. Bruce highlights this attitude summarized in the religious leaders' remarks in Acts 4:7: "By what power or name did you do this?" Bruce says, "There is a scornful emphasis in the position of the pronoun you *(humeis)* at the end of verse 7: 'people like you.' "[3] The religious leaders had extensive educations and superior positions in the community. They assumed they were the pious leaders, and if God would bless the people through anyone, it must be through them.

Our attitudes today can be remarkably similar. We assume that the power of God travels along the lines of educational degrees and sheer length of time spent as a Christian. It offends us when those who have done less than we have—especially in education and service—are seeing more blessing than we. Some of us may brag that we have had forty years of Christian experience, when in reality we may have had only one year of experience—repeated forty times.

I have seen new Christians do powerful feats in evangelism, healings and exercising gifts of the Holy Spirit. Their spiritual life is still young and the fruit of the Spirit is in bud, but God still entrusts gifts to them. This can make others uptight. "If this is from God, why is he not using *me? What's wrong with me?"* This kind of protest can be interpreted as: "There is nothing wrong with me—I have nothing to repent for, so this could not possibly be from God."

I have been guilty of this attitude myself. When my wife and several members of my church were filled with the Holy Spirit, I was very offended at first. Instead of rejoicing, I was outraged. Why was *I* passed over? What made *them* so special? Revival of spiritual life offended first-century religious leaders, and Satan will see to it that it offends every generation like them.

Jealousy

People may become jealous when they are not used as instruments in this new work. One of the leaders in the Catholic charismatic movement has said, "The charismatic movement is not too emotional; the problem is that it is too personal." This was certainly the case in Acts. Look at the contrast between the religious leaders and the apostles. These unschooled and ordinary men got to do miracles. They received the Spirit. They gathered the crowds. They were leading in revived worship, praying every day, and meeting the physical needs of the poor (Acts 2:42-47). Although it does not say so in the text, we can assume, based on our knowledge of the human heart, that the religious leaders were quite jealous.

I have seen this drama played out in local churches many times. I think of Sally and Rose, good friends who did many things together. Sally tried to get Rose to come to church with her on many occasions, but was not very successful. Then almost overnight, Rose was renewed in spiritual vigor. She began to do things that Sally, in all her long years of experience, never was able to do. Immediately Sally began to feel jealous and question why God would so bless Rose, when it was Sally who had been so faithful. Sally felt surges of unworthiness and wanted to give up. I am pleased to say Sally did recover, but it took some effort. And it was a rather unpleasant learning experience for her flesh.

Unpopular Principles

Revival confirms principles which the religious leaders are not prepared to embrace. The very evidence of the healed man in the Acts 4 account, done in the name of the resurrected Jesus, was contradictory to everything these leaders believed and taught. After all, it could not be right if it contradicted their stated theology. For example, the Sadducees, whose members came from the priestly line, and who controlled the temple, did not believe in the resurrection of the dead—particularly a man they had helped put to death. They did not believe they had done anything wrong in crucifying Jesus. But three times Peter makes it known to them that they were responsible for killing God's Anointed One. The leaders had refused to believe Jesus was Lord and Christ of Israel. As we have already said, it was not part of the leaders' understanding that ordinary people could ever do the work of God.

When I became involved in spiritual renewal, there were many things I did not believe because I had not seen them in Scripture. That does not mean, however, they weren't there. One reason I could not see them is because they were not in the realm of my experience. For example, I had not seen anyone healed by prayer alone. I had a general idea that it was possible, but I had no plan for cooperating with God to see it happen. I did not believe Christians could be demonized until I saw a clearly born-again pastor set free of multiple demons. I did not believe in prophecy or in words of knowledge until I began to work with men and women who seemed to "read my mail." Through God's promptings, they revealed the secrets of my heart (1 Cor 14:25). I was experiencing a "paradigm shift."[4] As I opened myself up to change, new experiences based upon the Scripture were coming true in my life.

Happy, Fearless and in Trouble

F. R. Maltby said Jesus promised his disciples three things: "They would be absurdly happy, completely fearless, and in constant trouble."[5] This is still our promise today. To think we can do anything significant for God and not encounter trouble is to believe a fairy tale. The principle is well established in Scripture, especially in the birth narrative of Jesus (Mt 2:13-18). At Jesus' birth, children were slaughtered in Bethlehem as the enemy made a savage assault to stop God's work. If Jesus could not enter the world without conflict, neither will we, if we maintain the vigor of Jesus' life in us.

There are no neat and tidy renewals in the Holy Spirit, as surely as there are no clean stalls when oxen are present (Prov 14:4). There will always be trouble. Satan will rage. People will be ill-informed. Others will be offended because they have not experienced the renewing work. Others will have their cherished beliefs challenged, and still others will be jealous because God has not chosen to use them. If we expect these responses, then we will understand the methods of the devil and thus be prepared to disarm his assaults when they come.

13 Give the Boy a Second Chance!

KALAFI MOALA WAS A YOUNG TONGAN BELIEVER WHEN HE first met Loren Cunningham, the director of Youth With A Mission.[1] Together they were witnessing door-to-door in a difficult Polynesian neighborhood in Auckland, New Zealand. Loren was so impressed with Kalafi that he invited him to join YWAM's South Pacific ministry. Several years later, however, Kalafi's life began to unravel. He had bouts with alcoholism and adultery, and eventually his marriage fell apart.

Attempts were made to see him restored, but he rebuffed each of these. In spite of his response, believers, sensing the heart of God, began to intercede for Kalafi's restoration. The cry was coming from heaven, "Somebody give the boy a second chance!" Several years later, after significant rehabilitation, Kalafi was re-established in the Lord and, eventually, to the directorship of YWAM's ministry in Southeast Asia.

Kalafi's life is a good example of spiritual warfare against young leaders and the process of seeing them reclaimed for kingdom work. The New Testament tells a very similar story about a young man named John Mark. After failing in another way, he was given a second chance and became a significant leader. As the story develops, notice the demonic purpose in this spiritual battle. The enemy wanted to bring confusion among co-workers so that a young man would be lost to ministry.

John Mark Strikes Out

Although little is known about most of the leaders in the early church, we know much about the life of John Mark. Mark was the son of Mary and was raised in a wealthy home which was used as a center of activity for the early church (Acts 12:12-13). Some suggest his home was the place of the Last Supper, and the place of the prayer room where the apostles met just before Pentecost (1:13). We know Mary had at least one servant, Rhoda, and a home of the size needed to accommodate a prayer room probably had more. If the owner of the Passover home was Mark's father (Mk 14:14), then we can conclude he probably died sometime after the crucifixion and before Peter's escape from prison (Acts 12:12). Documents outside of the New Testament refer to Mark as being "stumpy fingered." If this reflects his appearance, and not his writing style, then he was probably of a small and insignificant frame, with tiny hands. In summary, we might describe John Mark as a kid from a wealthy and active Christian home that was full of servants, and with a slight body deformity. But John Mark's life is really noted for the early trouble he encountered.

John Mark traveled with Barnabas and Saul as a "helper," a job which may not have suited his liking (Acts 12:25; 13:5). The term *helper* is used of an armed servant, an assistant in a synagogue, and of a rower on a Roman slave ship. In his job, Mark probably took care of the meals, the travel arrangements and any errands the two older men needed. Paul may have been unwell some of the time, so Mark may have also needed to nurse Paul's health (Gal 4:12-14). Whatever his specific duties, Mark was on call for the apostles and ran any errands they needed.

John Mark, however, left Paul and Barnabas in Cyprus at the beginning of their first missionary journey (13:13). The word for *left* in this verse is actually *deserted*. This abandonment had some major consequences. Why did John Mark leave? We are not told from the text, but I can suggest several possible reasons. It may have been one of these or a combination of all four.

Mark did not like the work of a servant. He was the rich kid who had been served by others and was not used to serving anyone. It disturbed him to be getting things for others rather than being served himself. But one of the principles of the kingdom of God is that we must be worker-servants before we can be leader-servants. If we cannot serve by working, we cannot serve by leading.

Mark may not have liked the leadership of the team. Notice that before the missionary journey began, it was Barnabas and Saul who were called (12:25). Barnabas is the one who goes and brings Saul back to Antioch (11:25). It is Barnabas who is named first in the prophetic call (13:2), and it is Barnabas's home turf of Cyprus that they are evangelizing (13:4). But a little further on in chapter 13, we see that Paul is recognized as the leader (v. 13). This may have been particularly offensive to Mark since he and Barnabas were cousins (Col 4:10). Mark's loyalty was reserved for Barnabas. He found it difficult to follow Paul, so he left. Paul may not have been totally innocent in the matter, but I believe that Mark had lessons to learn from Paul, lessons he aborted and had to learn later.

The approach of the team may not have been to Mark's liking. It is speculated in some scholarly circles that Mark's desertion was due to the fact that he, like the Judaizers, did not like Paul's approach to the Gentiles, especially in the matters of circumcision and ritual cleansing. In fact, Mark's return to Jerusalem and subsequent report of the mission *may* have been the leading cause for the convening of the Jerusalem Council (Acts 15:1-29). If this was the case, no wonder Paul was upset when he returned! The entire nature of the Gentile mission was being undercut by one who was formerly a member of his team.

Mark had seen plenty of conflict surrounding the gospel, and he was afraid. He was there the night Jesus was taken away, and found himself running naked into the dark after Jesus' captors tried to seize Mark too (Mk 14:51). Mark was there when Peter was arrested and when the persecution of believers became widespread (Acts 8:1; 12:1). In Cyprus, he saw Paul put a blinding curse on Elymas, the advisor to the proconsul Sergius Paulus (13:6-12). These events did not suggest a very secure future, and John Mark was afraid. This is not surprising, for hanging around the apostles was dangerous business.

Split Decision
Whatever the reason for Mark's departure, we know Paul refused to bring John Mark along on the second missionary journey (15:36-39). Paul may have been logistically correct, but I believe he missed in his discernment of Mark. He seems to have assumed that Mark had a major character flaw, but it was probably only a minor problem which could have been corrected. But Paul, at this point, failed to see the value of giving Mark a second chance.

When Paul rejected Mark, it was up to cousin Barnabas, the "son of encouragement," to take Mark under his wing (4:36; 15:39). We see from the Acts account that it seems to have been the right combination. As they traveled, they almost certainly talked about Paul. Possibly they talked about theology. And they must have discussed Mark's aversion to being a servant, since the one who did not like to serve eventually wrote Mark, the gospel with the servant focus. His weakness became his strength. This on-the-road discipleship, along with the paternal relationship Peter had with Mark, gave him a second chance and transformed him into a major leader in the early church.

How and when it happened we do not know, but Paul and Mark were restored in their appreciation for one another (Col 4:10; 2 Tim 4:11;

Philem 24). Because of it, the Christian church has a significant model for reconciliation. No doubt a process of time was needed for both Paul and Mark to reassess the situation and repent. All along, the heart of God was surely pressing both men about the oneness of the body of Christ. How could they preach the removal of barriers if they themselves were estranged from one another (Eph 2:14)?

Lessons of Reconciliation

Several principles of spiritual warfare apply to this biography and to ours. *This is not another story about personality differences.* We could surely show multiple psychological reasons for the conflict between Paul and Mark, but the thesis of this book is that spiritual opposition is not all ghostly faces and strange voices. Spiritual warfare comes in the normal course of human relationships, even relationships dedicated to building the kingdom of God. As a young Christian, I had a conflict with a particular leader. The matter was discussed by my elders, and their conclusion was "simply a matter of personality differences." I believed their conclusion for years—until I began to understand spiritual warfare. My elders had not taken the time, nor exercised the spiritual discernment, to know the true source of our conflict. We should never summarize conflict as simply "personality" without contending with the primary source as spiritual warfare.

The purpose of the enemy, especially among younger leaders, is to damage them early in their careers. Most often this comes through a relationship with an older leader who fails them at some point. The conflict damages the younger leader's assessment of God and the church. They reel for months or even years, as though they had been shot by a stun gun, under the impact of disillusionment. I have seen young leaders agonize over the lack of integrity shown toward them. They felt abused and wounded by the way they were treated. Many of them are today lost to the institutional church because of this harsh treatment.

When we began Grace Vineyard, God spoke to my wife and assured her that one of our ministries would be the restoration of young leaders. As soon as the church began, this word started to be fulfilled. Seminary graduates and former pastors began to arrive, all sharing the same story. These were not perfect, sinless people, just disillusioned former leaders who felt Christian ministry was full of charlatans and ungracious people. As with John Mark, most of them are now being restored.

The devil will exploit our inability to serve and to submit to one another. To serve and submit strikes at the very heart of our selfishness. Yet submission is the sign of the Spirit's filling, and service the mark of the disciple (Jn 13:12-17; Eph 5:18-21).

Mike was one of the most unusual pastors I have ever known. When we first met, he was a young man who had just returned from a short-term overseas project. He soon developed a relationship with an older pastor who was in need of help. Mike described his job this way: "I am my pastor's servant and helper. Whatever will make his job easier, I want to do. No job is too menial for me." Mike is a bright and capable fellow, and he might have wanted to spend his time learning all about preaching and counseling. But Mike's primary motive was not his own gain. He had come to serve and submit. Eventually, he took over many duties of the senior pastor, not because he plotted to have them, but because his service and submission made him the best qualified for the job.

The enemy will exploit inappropriate responses to leaders. It may happen that we disagree with the direction our leader is taking. While our concern may be legitimate, it is in our response that the enemy wants to drive a dividing wedge. Do we take our concern to our leader in trust that he will hear us, respecting his authority? Or do we give in to the temptation to sow dissension among the people, even to the point of splitting the fellowship? If the issue cannot be resolved, we need to leave peacefully. But there is no virtue in persuading others to join us. The enemy loves to see these kinds of pointless divisions take place. Trying to stop a leader with whom we disagree is not a priority of kingdom work.

Jesus took time to see Peter restored after he had denied him three times

(Mt 26:69-75; Jn 21:15-19). It seems appropriate, then, for all trainers to restore leaders who have sinned. I am not referring to the cheap grace that has been extended to fallen television evangelists or adulterous pastors. Even a leader like Kalafi Moala went through a lengthy process to be restored to his leadership. In certain traditions, major sins eliminate pastors from being restored to ministry. I have sympathy with this position, but I do not think it speaks from the heart of the gospel.

The healing of a restored leader takes time. It is not a quick fix. Many pastors who have lost their leadership positions are like drug addicts who crave their fix of approving strokes from the Sunday-morning crowd. Denying them this emotional boost sends them into the shakes. They do not know what to do with themselves or where to get the approval they desperately need. They must be given time to wean themselves from their "emotional drugs," time to heal the flaws which caused the problem in the first place, before they return to publicly leading people. Loving and discerning supervision must be lavished on these fallen leaders who are getting this kind of healing.[2]

Hasty judgments will keep many from entering the ministry. Frequently we are quick to write people off, refusing to give them a second chance. In our immaturity, we may assume that they are being disloyal to us and our values, and that it would be better to have them gone. But people have progressive learning curves and are capable of repenting in the right atmosphere. Our failure to understand this works against us as well as them. The heart of God is always open to giving a second chance.

Terry Lamb helped me to learn this lesson. When Terry joined our church staff as an intern, we were all excited about the ministry he would have with youth. Over the next two years, however, it became apparent that his ministry with the youth was not very successful. We began to question: "Why did we choose Terry in the first place?" He was supervised and seemed to be learning, yet there was little output. We came very close to letting Terry go, which would have frustrated both him and ourselves. At the same time, we had the deep sense that Terry was very gifted and had an important part to play in our fellowship. A second chance was in order. Today Terry is a capable pastor, and we would be thrilled to have him minister in our church. If we had gone with our first urge to let Terry go and not given him a second chance, the devil would have used us to bury a significant kingdom worker.

Time eventually heals all conflicts, if our hearts are open to the Lord. I learned this principle from a friend who was hurt badly in the latter part of his life. He was eased out of a church which he had grown. Yet he kept his heart open to the ones who had inflicted pain, and he believed reconciliation was possible. As my friend predicted, he was eventually restored to the people who had been his enemies.

Although I am fully aware that sinful and self-centered pastors daily plunder the flock of God, my appeal is that we should not bail out on the leaders God has given us. Surely cardinal sins like abuse, fraud and adultery are not to be tolerated without discipline, but each time we leave those who are appointed by God as our shepherds, we only delay learning the lesson God has placed in our path.

If we have been overlooked by Christian leaders and not given the second chance we want, then we need to begin our side of the healing by forgiving. We must forgive their impatience, their lack of grace, and their inability to see the anointing God has put in our lives. We need to ask God to give us a second chance, and to change the heart of the leader, so that we can be and do all God has made us for. We need also to give our leaders a second chance. We need to let them be the person we could gladly work with.

Mercy-Givers

This very minute there are men and women, pastors and laypeople, who need to be given a second chance. They have been written off for legitimate reasons of discipline as well as minor infractions and personality differences. Whether or not there was any formal statement creating a breach, emotionally they feel separated. At the same time the devil is waging war over their lives. He wishes these wounded soldiers to be rendered ineffective for the rest of their lives.

It is incumbent upon leaders to be like the father of the prodigal son (Lk 15:11-32), not only looking for the return of the lost son, but examining himself to see if he has done anything to encourage their leaving. The cry of heaven which launched intercession for Kalafi—"Somebody give the boy a second chance!"—is echoed today for the many leaders who need to be restored to ministry. And these second-chance believers, like John Mark, have shown that they have something to contribute to the church. We must not lose them in the battle.

14 Glory, Sex and Money

THE DEVIL IS A WORTHY ADVERSARY AND NEEDS TO BE treated with respect. He is not as dumb as we would make him out to be, but he does seem to be rather uncreative in the way he tempts Christian leaders. He has few new tricks, so he is content to use the same strategies which have worked so successfully in the past. I am referring to the old hat trick of glory, sex and money. Without any effort, I can list several dozen Christian leaders who have fallen through one of these temptations. We can resist Satan's old tricks by equipping ourselves for these warfare assaults. As Louis Pasteur is supposed to have said, "Chance favors the prepared man."

Glory: Give It to Jesus
John uses the term *glory (doxa)* eighteen times in his Gospel. Six of these

references are relevant to our study.

Jesus did not need to seek his own glory or fame, for the Father was seeking it for him (Jn 5:41; 8:50). Glory came to Jesus because he pleased the Father, and the Father was disposed to freely give praise to his Son.

Glory, as affirmation and praise, is something each of us needs. In fact, we cannot live healthy and effective emotional lives without it. However, where it comes from and how we get it are two major questions we must answer. Again, the Father sought glory for Jesus, and thus he did not need to seek it for himself. Likewise, our glory has already been determined by God (Rom 8:30). As surely as we have been justified by faith, we can be confident God has already arranged our glorification in Christ.

With this heavenly hope there is an earthly manifestation, a first in-stallment of affirmation. *We perceive our future glory by the witness of our adoption.* The witness of the Spirit, the cry *"Abba,* Father" (Gal 4:6), is the same affirming experience Jesus had at his baptism; "You are my Son, whom I love; with you I am well pleased" (Lk 3:22). It was God's seal of approval on Jesus, and it will be the same for us (Jn 6:27). These affirming words arrest our demand for praise from men. Once we have tasted God's love and pleasure, then the consuming need to receive glory fades.

Christian leaders assume their positions for a variety of reasons. Most often they have a genuine encounter with Christ and a call to ministry. After a season of leadership and some time of reflection, however, most of us begin to perceive other compelling motives for our decision.

In the process of sanctifying leaders, God allows us to evaluate *who* and *what* we are working for. He gives us the opportunity to ask ourselves, "Who is getting the glory?" In those moments, we may discover dark clouds veiling the lofty intentions of our calling. We may see that human dynamics have controlled our lives for years. Some have used leadership as a means of gaining approval that a parent never gave in childhood. For others, it is an opportunity to show the world that they have made some-thing of themselves. Leading can give a sense of self-worth to those who feel they are unimportant if they are not in leadership. For some, the need for praise is a raging lust. When others are praised and we are passed over, our lust roars like a brush fire, consuming everything in its path. But Jesus, secure in the affirmation of his Father, did not need the praise of men to be comfortable with his identity. Neither will we when God's affirmation touches the roots of our lives.

Jesus had more to say on the subject of praise and glory: "How can you believe if you accept praise *[glory]* from one another, yet make no effort to obtain the praise *[glory]* that comes from the only God?" (Jn 5:44).

Self-glory hinders faith. When the glory of man is our goal, we are consumed with working hard to receive praise, instead of living by faith. The praise of men becomes our chief preoccupation, coloring our decisions and interpretation of life. Praise becomes our oxygen, without which we cannot survive. But in such an environment, it is impossible to receive the praise which flows from the heart of God (Heb 11:6).

In chapter eight I discussed my own struggle with self-ambition and the praise of men. This is a serious impediment for any Christian leader and a major area for repentance.

My generation of evangelical leaders is a group of well-trained scholars, pastors and parachurch workers, amazing in their resources. Our clearest shortcoming is not our ethics, nor our industry, but our lack of ongoing faith. We have historical and doctrinal faith, but struggle to have present and dynamic faith. We speak like theists, but behave like deists. We teach as though God were present and powerful, but live as though he were distant and inept. Why such a failing? Our first hindrance is a theological model which suppresses the work of the Holy Spirit in this age. But the second, and much more personal reason, flows from this principle: *If we are seeking our own glory, we will not have faith.* I conclude faith has been robbed from us because we long for the fame and praise of men. In fact, *a preoccupation with the praise of men may be the foremost addiction among Christian leaders.*

Jesus elaborates on the condition of self-glory: "He who speaks on his own does so to gain honor *[glory]* for himself" (Jn 7:18).

When we speak without reference to God's thoughts, either those of Scripture or those given by the Holy Spirit, then we are seeking our own glory. Persuasive arguments and eloquent speech, unaided by God's Spirit, are our own way of bringing attention to ourselves.

I remember hearing a well-known Welsh preacher spin the most elaborate and complicated sermon I have ever heard. But when it was over, there was no power in the application, nor in changed lives. He had all the intonations of revival preaching, but there was no power. The man was so thrilled with his own eloquence and with the glory it had brought him in the past that he failed to realize God was no longer anointing his words. Richard Baxter, a British chaplain from the seventeenth century, addresses this very theme in his classic work *The Reformed Pastor.*

Having prepared the sermon, pride then goes into the pulpit. It sets the tone, shapes the delivery, and strips away any offense, to gain the maximum applause. The end result is that it makes men both in studying and preaching seek their own self-interest, and after reversing worship roles, they deny God instead of glorifying God and denying themselves. Instead then of asking, "What shall I say, and how should I say it, to please God best, and do most good," pride makes them ask, "How shall I deliver it to be thought a learned, able preacher, and be applauded by all who hear me?"[1]

In John 17:22, Jesus talks about the place of glory: "I have given them the *glory* that you gave me, that they may be one as we are one." Jesus gives away his glory so that his disciples might be one. This glory is his presence, which when invited, allows us to be one. When he is present, we stop comparing and complaining, and begin to build up one another. In this way, leaders who realize they are honored by God have the security to prefer one another in love.

How should a Christian handle praise? When praise comes from God, through men, it is God's affirmation for us. We need to receive it, rejoice in it and enjoy it. God is saying we have done a good job, and he is building confidence in our lives. I remember when I, as a new Christian, gave my testimony at my home church. Afterwards, a well-respected seminary professor commented to a friend about me, "Someday he will make a good preacher." For years his comment gave me confidence that God could use me to communicate his love and truth.

There is another kind of praise, however. When glory is offered to us through flattery, excessive adulation or hero worship, we must resist. We resist by not letting these comments penetrate our spirits, by not embracing them, nor trying to make them our own. Ingesting such words only produces sickness: "It is not good to eat too much honey, nor is it honorable to seek one's own honor" (Prov 25:27).

The world encourages us to "blow our own horns." But self-glory evaporates like dew. Lasting glory comes only from the Father. Glory we give ourselves is worthless, but glory that comes from the Father we cannot lose. If we seek glory for God, he will seek ours. If we seek our own glory, we cannot have his. The praise of men is the devil's scheme to hide the glory of God and to prevent us from walking in faith. It is a subtle attack, unrecognizable to most, but it is a blow to the body of Christ every time a Christian leader acts out of wanting this kind of praise.

Sex: Reserved for Mates

If the devil cannot cause us to stumble over self-glory, he will try to trap us sexually. Great and small have fallen by this temptation. We are sexual people, and it is not helpful to repress this fact. Rather, we need to openly analyze this area of ourselves and our lives and respond straightforwardly to the biblical demands. A good starting point for biblical help is 1 Thessalonians 4:1-8.

Paul writes about avoiding sexual immorality, bodily self-control, being pure and holy. The instructions Paul shares came directly from the teaching of Jesus (v. 2). It was not an ascetic Paul who thought up notions of self-control, but a faithful servant passing along the words of his Master. The will of God for every person is that they should be set aside for holiness, or sanctified, both in this life and the life to come (v. 3). The death of Christ has in principle made us holy; therefore we are called *saints* or *holy ones* (Rom 1:7; Heb 10:10). But holiness is also to be pursued (Heb 12:14). One aspect of the pursuit is abstinence from immorality (1 Thess 4:3). This term covers a multitude of illicit sexual relationships or behaviors. Leon Morris comments on the necessity of this imperative:

> For the Greeks, sexual sins were lightly condemned. Continence was regarded as an unreasonable demand on a man. In society at large it was taken for granted that men would naturally seek the satisfaction of their sexual desires outside the marriage bond. The pressure to conform to the easy standards accepted throughout the society must have been strong on the early church. . . . Yet the leaders of the church did not compromise for one moment.[2]

To spell out the boundaries of abstinence may be stating the obvious, but experience tells me that in sexual matters we are better off not to take anything for granted. Christians, by virtue of their union with Christ and their practice of his commandments, will abstain from:

Adultery: Sexual relationships with another person's spouse or between a married person and an unmarried person (Ex 20:14).

Fornication: Sexual relationships between unmarried persons (Heb 13:4).

Incest: Sexual relationships with any member of the immediate family besides the marriage partner (Lev 18:6).

Pornography: Reading or viewing material whose primary purpose is sexual arousal.

Masturbation: Lustful self-stimulation of one's genitals to the point of orgasm. The Bible is silent on this issue, neither condoning nor condemning the practice. It is best seen as a sign of immaturity rather than as a transgression of some moral law. However, it is obviously wrong when associated with lust or habitual practices that cannot be stopped. *— fantasizing*

Prostitution: Paying for sexual relationships with someone other than our own mate (Prov 6:26; 1 Cor 6:15).

Homosexuality: Having sexual relationships with someone of the same sex (Rom 1:24-27).

Voyeurism: Covert spying on people for the purpose of sexual arousal.

Lustful thoughts: Patterns of thinking which have sexual lust as the focus (Mt 5:27-28).

Although there has been increasing pressure for some of these sexual acts to be permitted for Christians, the plain teaching of Scripture does not allow for this sexual sin.

Sexual control is a learned process. It takes discipline of mind and body. Such control is in the realm of possibility and thus expected of every Christian. If our sexual lives are out of control, then we are out of control. Such behavior is typical of those who do not know God, but is manageable for those who have been touched by the Spirit of God (1 Thess 4:4-5).

Holiness also requires that Christian brothers and sisters not sin against each other sexually. If a man sins against a woman in this way, he offends not only her, but the man she may one day marry (1 Thess 4:6). The biblical view of sex outside of marriage is that someone will be damaged by the practice, and sexual looseness is an injustice to more people than the two parties involved (Prov 6:20-27). Chaste sexual behavior is then compelled by three reasons: (1) God's purpose for us is holiness, not impurity (1 Thess 4:7); (2) God will avenge those who do not heed this warning (1 Thess 4:6); and (3) impurity is a sin against the teaching of the Holy Spirit (1 Thess 4:8).

Sexual control is not just a matter of mental and physical discipline; it is a matter of exercising godly wisdom and resisting the enemy. Reflecting upon my own background, I realize how ill equipped I was to handle matters of sexuality. Because I know that there are many others who are similarly ill equipped, I believe it will be helpful to share the following principles I have learned, in hopes that they will prove wise in contending with sexual temptation.[3]

Maintain a healthy and frequent sexual relationship with our mate. A pastor came to me with the conviction that he was demonized. I asked him why he thought so, and he told me of his patterns of lust and masturbation. So I asked about the frequency of intercourse he had with his wife. He responded, "Once or twice a month." I had expected him to say, "Once or twice a week." My reply was simple: "Friend, you don't have a demon problem, you have a marriage problem." Sexual intercourse in marriage is holy, and God encourages frequency in our union (Heb 13:4; 1 Cor 7:1-5). This frequency should be discussed by both parties, so that all needs are met and temptation is kept at a distance. Spiritualizing infrequency or neglecting conversations about the subject are mistakes that can play into the hands of the enemy. Happy lovers do not need new sexual partners.

Former President John F. Kennedy was a well-known womanizer, even while he was in office. He was once confronted by a friend who said, "Jack, you can eat a hamburger and a piece of pie in ten minutes, but you cannot make love to a woman in that time."

This is true and sobering advice even for Christian men. Good love-making is emotional and psychological long before it is physical. It is a matter of who we are rather than of what we do. Communication is the groundwork for sexual intercourse; the more we listen, the more likely we are to experience the intimacy we long for. Such tenderness should go on all day, from the morning leaving until the evening greeting. Affectionate acts must always precede sexual acts, and emotional tenderness will come before physical touch. In this intimate environment, we need to constantly give and receive forgiveness, insuring no roots of bitterness are growing. Good love-making can happen when two people have the physical energy to pay attention to what they are doing. Many sexual relationships bog down with protests of fatigue. Once sexual intimacy has begun, communication is the best way to determine if we are fully pleasing our mates.

Name any sexual problem we have, confessing it to a close friend or mate. A number of years ago, I met with a group of men on a weekly basis, much like early Methodist band meetings. Pornography had been an issue for some of these brothers, so we made a pact with each other, based upon James 5:16, to confess our sins and pray for each other. Each session began with confessing our sins to one another and receiving forgiving prayer. Their enemy became our adversary, and their fight became our battle. Such accountability broke the back of the addiction which had plagued these brothers.

Recognize that lust is subject to the law of diminishing returns. The more we get, the more we want. Conversely, the less we get, the less we want. Moving to a higher and more intense level of lust—like from fantasy to visual pornography—will leave us unsatisfied thereafter with anything less than the higher level, and unable to return to a lower one. The only way to destroy lust is to stop feeding it. If it has no food, it cannot grow. If we starve it long enough, it will go away.

Trace the history of our sexual lust, discovering where it began and why we act it out. A youth worker came to me confessing masturbation and pornography. I asked him when and where he masturbated. "In my bedroom, about three o'clock in the afternoon," he said. "Why are you in bed at three o'clock in the afternoon?" was my reply. He went on to explain how his ministry went late into the night, and that's why he needed an afternoon nap. I told him that personal ministry was not only spiritual but emotionally intimate, and potentially sexual. His late arrival home meant that his wife and children were asleep—hence, he was having no intimacy with his wife. This was what had produced the pattern of "solo sex." Once I explained the cycle and he was able to adjust his lifestyle, he no longer had a problem.

Demythologize sexual affairs of the mind. Affairs never live up to what we imagine in our dreams. Illicit relationships must still contend with unromantic moments and the realities of life. The man still has smelly socks, and the woman, rollers in her hair. Once the excitement is gone, life is no better than what it was at home. We need to remind ourselves of this, speaking out loud when necessary.

Confess the real price we pay for acting out our lust. For me, sexual lust produces anger. If I have lustful intentions, I can be assured that anger, particularly at my family, will follow. But there are other consequences for acting out lust. We can expect a guilty conscience when we transgress God's laws. If our sin becomes known, we will suffer public disgrace. And finally, in a day when AIDS can be contracted through casual sex, our very lives could be at stake.

Recognize the humanity of those we lust after. Often, these are brothers and sisters in the kingdom, and if not, we must remember at least that they are creations of God. They are real people, and the more we comprehend their humanity, the less likely we will be to make them objects of our lust.

Avoid sexually seductive speech. "I can talk to you easier than any other person I know" may sound innocent enough, but in the wrong context it can be an invitation to further intimacy and sexual contact.

Flee vulnerable relationships. On more than one occasion when sexual innuendos were flying in the room, I have taken myself by the back of the neck and run as quickly as possible. We should feel free to leave a questionable situation promptly, not worrying about being proper. We do not fight sexual temptation by standing and resisting, but by running (1 Cor 6:18).

Counter sexual temptations with productive activities. We need to put time, energy and money into positive activities which can take our attention off of our temptations. In this way, we fill up our lives so that temptation has no time to be fulfilled. In addition, I occasionally recommend a little behavior modification for simple addictions. I place a quarter-inch rubber band on the wrist of the person and tell them not to take it off until they return to see me again. I instruct them to pop themselves with the rubber band every time they are tempted by lustful thoughts or behavior. It sounds simple, but thirty days of such conditioning does halt some addictions.

Persistently acknowledge God's forgiveness for sexual sins. It is the enemy's lie which says God cannot forgive a repeated sexual sin. Even though we may sin, confess and sin again, there is no corner so dark that God's forgiving grace cannot come to the truly repentant.

Only the pure in heart will see God (Mt 5:8). If we truly want to live in the realm of God's presence, we need to walk in sexual purity. And once we have tasted this realm, we will know the inferiority of anything less.

Abiding by these principles is one way of giving no place to the devil. They serve as safety fences against the enemy's attacks. The practices in and of themselves, however, do not guarantee that the devil will not launch a sexual siege against us. There are seasons when undue temptations do come, even to the most disciplined soldier. Therefore, we must be ever watchful, trusting not in our self-discipline alone, but in God who provides our way of escape (1 Cor 10:13).

Money: For Kingdom Purposes

If the devil fails to defeat leaders through glory or sex, he will try to succeed through the abuse of money. The following guidelines are helpful in remaining above reproach regarding money (1 Tim 3:2).

If covetousness can disqualify us from inheriting the kingdom of God, it also ought to disqualify us from being a Christian leader (1 Cor 6:9-10; 1 Tim 3:2-3). The great majority of full-time Christian leaders live with a minimal salary (hopefully, the principle that the worker should receive a fair wage is being observed—1 Tim 5:18) and a simple lifestyle. There is, however, a growing trend which says that leaders deserve large homes and expensive cars. This is advocated as a right as well as a blessing. Many leaders who fall into this way of thinking come from economically poor backgrounds, and they have had little instruction in handling money. Unfortunately, it does not take long for the love of money and the consuming desire for affluence to take control. Such desire must disqualify men and women from leading the church.

In order to bring no hindrance to the gospel, Paul refused to accept financial support from those who directly received his ministry (1 Cor 9:3-18; 2 Cor 11:7-9). Paul had such a right and advocated it for others, but did not receive it himself. He went out of his way to separate a free gospel and the means by which he made a living. He saw his tentmaking as a practical response to any suggestion that he may have been a preacher for money. Today, we cannot watch religious television without hearing repeated pleas for money. The purpose of such telecasts, say these evangelists, is to reach the lost. Yet they have woven a free gospel into a pay message. Even non-Christians with no particular religious insight know something is wrong with this practice.

Although Paul did not raise his own financial support, he had no qualms in aggressively doing it for other people (2 Cor 8—9). Paul was a fund raiser, but never for himself. Nothing hindered him from appealing for the needs of others, but he never mentioned his own needs to those he ministered to. By contrast, many parachurch agencies demand that their staff go cap-in-hand in search of financial support. My own conviction is that this approach discourages a life of faith and puts the worker in a vulnerable relationship with the donor. Such an arrangement means the severing of finances if the worker does not please the donor. Therefore, the sin of many agencies is to live at the wishes of their constituencies. If money needs to be raised, we ought to let others serve as our advocates rather than ourselves.

Finances in the kingdom need to be handled through credible and accountable means (2 Cor 8:16-24). In the early days of his ministry, Billy Graham was caught by a newspaper photographer, carrying bags of money from his crusade. This picture, which had wide circulation, taught the young evangelist the hard lesson of avoiding evil, even in appearance. Graham learned from this event and has over the years been one of the leading spokesmen for financial integrity. It is not necessary to tie the hands of Christian workers so that they cannot respond quickly to financial needs; nor is it helpful to allow them exclusive and unaccountable control over finances. Checks and balances are proper, as long as the motivation is to release funds into the kingdom, not to conserve them.

Phil was a fifth-grade friend and fellow player on our school basketball team. Along with his other attributes, he had a particular gesture which I have never forgotten. Whenever he scored a goal or did something clever on the court, he always had a smirking smile of pride. Even as a ten-year-old, I recognized his response to the praise of men.

I see Christian leaders today with similar gestures. And when this sign of pride appears, along with expensive lifestyles and attractive companions, we can be assured the devil has baited his trap. It is a sad tragedy when these leaders fall, not only for them but also for the sheep whom they have disappointed. This picture I paint is not so remote. No leader is above a fall. But the leaders who will stand are those who have prepared well. Louis Pasteur spoke of chance favoring the well-prepared man. From a perspective of spiritual warfare, we may reword his advice to say: "Satan is hindered by the prepared man."

15 Trouble at the Wall

HAVE YOU EVER READ *THE LITTLE ENGINE THAT COULD* BY Watty Piper? It's the account of a little steam engine which comes to the rescue of a big, shiny, broken-down train. The little engine is called to aid in the urgent mission of carrying toys to the children over the mountain. Although the load is heavy and the hills steep, the little engine conquers every challenge by repeating to himself, "I *think* I can, I *think* I can."

In the book of Nehemiah, Israel is much like the little engine, carrying a heavy load. But instead of being buoyed up by optimistic determination, they are weighed down by negative skepticism. The people of Judah were saying, "The strength of the laborers is giving out, and there is so much rubble that we cannot rebuild the wall" (Neh 4:10). In other words, Israel was repeating to itself, "We *don't think* we can, we *don't think* we can."

Why such pessimism? Nehemiah learned from his brother that the Jews who had returned to Jerusalem after the Babylonian captivity were in great distress (1:1-3). The walls of the city were broken down, so the inhabitants were defenseless in the face of attack. Nehemiah secured permission from King Artaxerxes to go to Jerusalem and lead in the rebuilding of the wall (2:1-8). Israel's enemies were not pleased at this show of strength, so they discouraged the worker and attempted to intimidate the people at every opportunity. They incited so much opposition to the wall's rebuilding that the Israelites themselves began to doubt the value of their task and their ability to see it completed. Nehemiah stood firm, however, and succeeded in encouraging the people by his own reliance on God.

While we today are not concerned with rebuilding a literal wall, there is much we can learn from the book of Nehemiah. *It serves as a primer in spiritual warfare for Christian leaders.*[1]

A Burdened Heart

Spiritual warfare began for Nehemiah when he heard of the great trouble and disgrace in Jerusalem (1:3). This news overwhelmed him, and he responded by weeping, mourning, fasting and praying for many days (1:4). Plaguing Nehemiah's heart was the question his opposition raised about the Jews: "Can they revive the stones from the dusty rubble, even the burnt ones?" (4:2 NASB). In other words, can there be revival in the midst of devastation? The Hebrew word for *revive* refers to life being restored to the dead. The same term is used of reviving the widow's son (1 Kings 17:21-23), of the dead man who came back to life when he was thrown upon the grave bones of Elisha (2 Kings 13:21), and in the psalmist's plea for Israel, "Will you not revive us again, that your people may rejoice in you?" (Ps 85:6). We now understand why this story is about spiritual warfare: *Nehemiah was praying for revival.* His vision was for a restored wall, a functioning temple, and a people passionate for the heart of God. His burden was so overwhelming that he fasted and prayed to ask God to restore his people.

How about ourselves? Have we seen the devastation the enemy has reaped in the world and in the church? I remember the first time God placed on my heart the burden of a renewed church. Until then, I had had no idea that the church was in need of revival. It seemed fine to me. I was learning many wonderful things in the church and meeting some of the finest people I had ever known.

Before long, however, I began to see that nominalism in the church had dulled the radical claims of Jesus. People were rearranging the deck chairs, but the *Titanic* was still going down. Religious vocabulary camouflaged the reality of the devastation. One leader said, to explain the slide in his denomination's attendance, "Our church is not dying, it is dieting." But there is a world of difference between dieting and anorexia. Some churches, with their liberal theologies and practices, seem to want to fold up their tents and give their business over to psychologists and social workers. Other churches, hiding behind claims of proper doctrine, seem to be no better off, for they appear to have lost their first love (Rev 2:4). When I began to see these things, God's burden for revival was birthed in me.

God's Values

Resurrection is no effort for God. His only problem is to get us to lay down and admit that we are dead. Only God can permit us to see the devastation in the church, to feel it in our hearts, and to pray for a revived church. Therefore, it should not be any surprise that the *enemy attacks by blinding our eyes so that we cannot see the devastation which is in the church.* He also wants us to be passive about changes which could lead to revival.

I have often spoken and written on the subject of revival. What puzzles me is how indifferent people tend to be on the subject. In 1983, I toured seventeen Canadian cities, listening to what pastors and churches were doing in each locale. In each city I preached from Psalm 85:6, "Revive Us Again." But few of my hearers seemed to see the devastation, let alone feel God's burden. They did not value sufficiently what God valued. This is why Nehemiah is such a unique man. He valued what God valued, and what was in God's heart was in Nehemiah's. Although the Jews in Jerusalem were aware of the devastation, they could not see its significance because they did not have the heart of God.

The intention of the enemy is to keep us ignorant of the devastation of the church in our midst and helpless to do anything about it. He wants to keep us from valuing what is in God's heart. Therefore, if we are to see the enemy defeated, we must begin by understanding God's heart and purpose. Nehemiah's response to Israel's devastation is an excellent example.

Ask God for a spirit of illumination. We need revelation from the Holy Spirit to perceive where and how God is moving, and to know the concerns of his heart. His agenda—that his glory would be seen in all the nations—has not changed (Ps 96:3). But God does his work in each nation and people according to his timing. By revelation, we ascertain where God is building and blessing. Nehemiah's prayer for favor in the king's eyes was his way of asking God to reveal if the timing was right to restore Jerusalem (Neh 1:11).

Acknowledge our lack of care for the devastation of the church and confess our failure to value what God values (2 Chron 7:14). God already knows we do not care about revival; he simply wants us to acknowledge it. We need to be ruthlessly honest with ourselves in confessing the state of our hearts to God. We are not to weep over how bad things are, but how badly we have failed to care for his work. When Nehemiah heard about the devastation of Jerusalem, *he had God's heart for the people and the city* (Neh 1:4). He did not ignore what he heard, nor did he try to give the responsibility to someone else. After he heard about the trouble and disgrace of the Jewish remnant, Nehemiah repented on behalf of his people for their failure to follow God and his laws (1:6-7).

Acknowledge that our choice is the major ingredient the Holy Spirit will use to cause us to value what God values. The Holy Spirit cooperates with our choice. He will not move on us if we are not prepared to move. Our choices to be open to God affect other people; as we change, others will be free to change. Nehemiah's choice to come before the Lord in confession and intercession for the people of Israel opened the path for God to move through him for the restoration of Jerusalem. He did not shirk the responsibility that God was calling him to on behalf of the Israelites. Although he was not personally involved in the sin of Israel, Nehemiah *assumed he was part of the problem for the devastation, and not just part of the solution* (1:6-7). Too often we make excuses for our noninvolvement, and claim that the church's devastation has nothing to do with us. When we see a need, it does not always mean God is calling us to actively remedy the situation, but we should value the situation in the same way God would.

Affirm by faith and action that God's Word is our solution (Ps 119). There are many clever plans for reviving the church, but only in God's Word are we assured of an unalterable remedy for the ills of the church. We follow his guidance because it is right, not because we feel like it; we do it because there is no other way the devastation can be overcome. As he intercedes for the Israelites, Nehemiah drew from God's covenant to the people of Israel. Based on God's Word, he was drawn into repentance and then was led to call on the promises of God for the deliverance of his people (Neh 1:5-9). He then asked God for his blessing and developed a plan of action to revive the devastation (1:11-2:8).

Countering Attacks

The late Billy Martin, who managed several baseball teams, including the New York Yankees and Oakland Athletics, gave this formula for leadership to *Sports Illustrated:* "You'll have fifteen guys who will run through a wall for you, five who hate you and five who are undecided. The trick is to keep the five who hate you away from the five who are undecided."[2] This is a man who had learned to spot his enemy and to defeat his plans.

Nehemiah also was a man who knew how to counter the attacks of his enemy. Once Nehemiah perceived Jerusalem's devastation, the enemy began to lay his plan of attack. Once he began to do something about the devastation, the enemy launched his attack. No sooner had Nehemiah started the revival process than he was *attacked by enemies from without, and confusion from within.* Nehemiah's response to these attacks is instructive to every leader who fights for the values of God.

His enemies mocked him and ridiculed his efforts (Neh 2:19; 4:1-3). When Nehemiah arrived in Jerusalem, he found he had stirred a hornet's nest. He was surrounded by opposition. Sanballat and his Samaritans were in the north, Tobiah and the Ammonites were in the east, Geshem the Arab was in the south, and the Ashdodites were in the west. Nehemiah was completely encircled by those who were displeased that anyone would care for the welfare of Israel. His enemies joked among themselves that if even a fox should jump on the newly constructed wall, it would certainly fall down. Their intention was to demoralize the workers with their ridicule.

When I was an InterVarsity staffworker, some students I was leading became demoralized by ridicule. It happened one evening when I was speaking at an evangelistic meeting in a dormitory. A surprise visitor showed up—Frank Herbert, the author of the popular novel *Dune* and a cult hero on many campuses. After my presentation, he and I began a rather vigorous debate. He was unwilling to respond to the facts of Christianity, focusing his attention instead on ridiculing the church and naming abuses done in the name of Christ. At that time, I was somewhat a seasoned staffworker, so his words did not penetrate me personally. However, when I looked at the Christian students who sponsored the event, I saw they were deeply absorbing his blows. Discouragement and doubt began to fall upon them like a blanket. Herbert's words were intended to produce skepticism, not illumination. His comments were devastating to these students, and hindered the progress of their Christian group for over a year.

In retrospect, I should never have entered into the debate without warning the students what was about to happen and arranging for a feedback session afterwards. Mature leaders often forget what ridicule can do to young believers. One comment by a reputed authority can send them into a tailspin. Rejection is a vital component in discipleship, but unprocessed rejection leads to defeat (Lk 10:16).

The enemy assaulted by encouraging some of the Jews to loaf on the job (Neh 3:5). These were wealthy aristocrats who disdained manual labor. As we can imagine, when they refused to work, morale on the entire project was damaged. Conflicting feelings arose as people compared what they produced next to what their noble neighbors managed to repair.

Likewise, the enemy plants in every church a few well-chosen pew-sitters. They believe they are above working, but not above having an opinion. These loafers plant themselves near the work, but only slow its progress. Things would go quite well without their contribution, but they seem to appear on influential committees, guaranteeing stalled decisions and conflicting relationships.

The enemy further hindered the work by sowing pessimistic rumors (4:10-12). As we have noted, word began to circulate that everyone was tired, there was too much to do, and the project would never be completed. As with most rumors, we are not privy to how this rumor in the book of Nehemiah got started, nor to the tracks it followed. Without the approval of Nehemiah, it spread throughout the city, gaining more authority with every whisper. But it was a lie—there was enough strength for the job, and the task was to be completed.

Every leader must give attention to communication with his people. People are always talking about their perception of the work, whether we give them permission to or not. Therefore, we need to keep communicating in order to clear the air of false notions. But as hard as we may try, we can be assured that the enemy will plant rumors to damage our progress. The only way rumors are halted is by clear and truthful communication coming from those in authority. It was once rumored that I was attempting to usurp the position of my senior pastor. With my forthright communication and a modeled response of love for my pastor, the slander eventually halted. Communication is not just for halting rumors, but also for motivating the troops (2:17). As Nehemiah spoke, people could see the devastation that they had previously ignored. They caught his clear perception of the heart of God. People are encouraged to work when they see the vision and assume partnership in that vision. "Come, let us build" evokes a response only from those who have a revelation of God's heart.

The enemy promoted internal conflicts (5:1-13; 6:17-19). In the midst of rebuilding, some of the wives came to Nehemiah with a concern. "Nehemiah, we have some news for you. We can't *eat* these rocks we're building with. And besides, this wall project of yours is just costing us too much." Nehemiah continued to listen to find out the source of this rather strong reaction. "You see, it's like this. Since we have been working on your wall, we have not been punching the time clock, so we have no money to pay the king's income tax. Then one of the good brothers, honest Ben, opened up a pawn shop, taking our property and kids in exchange for money to pay the king's tax." Nehemiah was incensed. Immediately he confronted Ben and demanded restitution for the people he had taken advantage of, and he stopped the usury (Ex 22:25).

Sadly, there are still believers who take advantage of the troubles of others. They pretend to help, but all along the benefits are for themselves. Various pyramid schemes flow through churches, making the poor poorer and the rich richer. I have seen Christians lose thousands of dollars through economic schemes which had no validity. The end result was what the enemy wanted—broken relationships and conflicts within the church.

This kind of manipulation can also happen in the emotional arena. A needy Christian seeks emotional help from a counselor who himself is needy. Soon a codependent relationship develops, compounding the person's trouble.

There was a second internal problem in Jerusalem surrounding Tobiah.

This man was a servant of the king of Amon (Neh 2:10) and one of the partygoers who had joked about Israel (4:3). He had business contacts with Jews and Jewish relatives through marriage (6:17-19). While Nehemiah was away, Tobiah pulled a few family strings and got himself a room in the temple (13:6-9). Slowly but surely, Tobiah began to infiltrate the Jews, turning them against Nehemiah.

In the same manner, an extended family can turn against a leader at the instigation of just one member. One offended person can insure that all his family members are apprised of the breach and the necessity of collective opposition. Therefore, family units can function as bastions for the enemy's intentions, promoting family loyalty over kingdom loyalty. Many leaders have fallen because of their conflict with an influential family.

The opposition to the revival intensified when the wall was half completed (Neh 4:6-8). Sanballat and his friends were particularly incensed when the gap in the wall was closed, and they began to plot a physical attack to match their verbal onslaught.

The enemy relishes in discouraging us at the half-way point. He wants us to believe we have wasted our labor on an unfinished project. He wants us to be discouraged through fatigue, guilt and condemnation. It may be that the midway point of any kingdom project is particularly vulnerable. Other assaults—blindness to need, lack of hope, lack of creativity—seem to appear at the beginning of projects.

At this midway point, Nehemiah redoubles his watchfulness and prepares for battle (4:13-23). From his example we learn that our response should be twofold: staving off the enemy by affirming our workers, and arming our workers for battle. Affirmation of our goals, purposes, and the contributions the workers make closes the gap. The enemy cannot disturb the flock when everyone is apprised of where they are going and what the plan is to get there. If they also know they are loved and appreciated, further protection surrounds them. As for our armament, we are to begin with an intense session of intercession, seeking the face of God for protection from our enemies. A season of intercession may last for months, or until we are advised we can stop.

Nehemiah is himself a model of such praying. Four times in the book he utters significant prayers. At the beginning of the mission, Nehemiah repented of Israel's sins and sought God's success in petitioning the king (1:4-11; 2:4). When his enemies were ridiculing his efforts, he called on God to return their insults upon their own heads (4:4-5; 6:14), and he continued to pray for strength that the job would be completed (6:9; 13:22, 29).

Occasionally the enemy tempts us to leave the work altogether (6:1-4). Nehemiah was invited to the plain of Ono for a discussion. But he knew Sanballat's crew only meant him harm. Nehemiah's response was simple and still valid today, "Ono, I can't go." Nehemiah knew what his priorities were and was not intimidated into attending a meeting he knew he shouldn't be at.

For anyone doing the work of God, there are always debaters and critics who want to use up our time just to analyze what is going on. Such people are often enemy agents sent to halt our progress. I have seen it in graduate students who are writing papers, reporters who want our comments, and the ever-present expert on church life, who wants to know what we think. Seldom if ever do these consultations further our goals, and most often they are a hindrance. We are best to stay clear of such distractions and keep ourselves focused upon the work.

Nehemiah is an excellent model of a spiritual warrior, and it is good to internalize the lessons we learn from him. First of all, whenever God allows us to see the devastation of the church and to feel his heart for it, we can anticipate enemy opposition. It is essential at this point to spiritually discern where and how the enemy is attempting to keep us from following God's heart for his church.

Once we have begun to bring revival, we must teach our flock to handle rejection from those who would ridicule our work. We need to be aware of spiritual loafers who slow down God's work, and remove them from positions of authority. We need to communicate with our flock, spelling out goals for all to hear and dispelling rumors. We will need to monitor potential internal problems, particularly when one person is preying upon another. We will need to encourage kingdom loyalty as superior to family loyalty, breaking up unhealthy family controls. We need to intensify our affirmation of people and our commitment to prayer, especially at the halfway point of any kingdom venture. Last, we must reject any pandering to our pride which distracts us from the work and which would cause us to abandon the building process of revival.

On April 19, 1990, I completed the sixth draft of *Arming for Spiritual Warfare*. There was a sense of relief and fulfillment as I went to lunch that day. Two hours later I received a phone call telling me "a hundred people are leaving your church." The elders and I were caught off guard, having had no forewarning of any problems that would provoke such an exodus.

I am not a perfect pastor and make mistakes all the time. Surely my inadequacy contributed to some of the exodus, and for this I feel both shame and pain.

At the same time, I find it suspicious to have had such a conflict only two hours after I finished a book on spiritual warfare. This is just like our enemy—to find a weakness in me or in one of my congregation and to exploit it for all it is worth. Yet, in spite of this apparent defeat, we are learning about spiritual warfare and how shrewd our enemy really is. Still, we are having our share of victories and are taking territory daily.

Praise God! Bonnie is still alive.

Bonnie died Nov. 22, 1991

God is being glorified through her life... and death, as she asked, that He would have a "heyday" with this.

Notes

Preface
[1]Jessie Penn-Lewis, *War on the Saints* (Fort Washington, Penn.: Christian Literature Crusade, 1977).
[2]Michael Green, *I Believe in Satan's Downfall* (Grand Rapids, Mich.: Eerdmans, 1981), p. 42.

Chapter 1: Introduction: Beyond Screwtape
[1]C. S. Lewis, *The Screwtape Letters* (New York: Macmillan Company, 1961).
[2]From Martin Luther's hymn "A Mighty Fortress Is Our God."
[3]Mark Kilroy, a twenty-one-year-old student at the University of Texas, was killed in such a way. *Brownsville Herald* (April 12, 1989).
[4]George Eldon Ladd, *A Theology of the New Testament* (Grand Rapids, Mich.: Eerdmans, 1974), p. 51.
[5]Ibid., p. 66.
[6]Michael Green, *I Believe in Satan's Downfall* (Grand Rapids, Mich.: Eerdmans, 1981).
[7]Frank Peretti, *This Present Darkness* (Westchester, Ill.: Crossway Books, 1986) and *Piercing the Darkness* (Westchester, Ill.: Crossway Books, 1989).
[8]From the hymn "A Mighty Fortress Is Our God."

Chapter 2: Choose Your Weapons
[1]John R. W. Stott, *The Message of Ephesians* (Downers Grove, Ill.: InterVarsity Press, 1979), p. 262.
[2]*Oxford English Dictionary.*
[3]Johannes P. Louw and Eugene A. Nida, eds., *Greek-English Lexicon of the New Testament: Based on Semantic Domains,* 2 vols. (New York: United Bible Societies, 1988), 1:74.7.

[4]Markus Barth, *Ephesians 4—6,* The Anchor Bible (Garden City, N.Y.: Doubleday, 1974), p. 762.

[5]Michael Green develops a heavenly and earthly description of powers in *I Believe in Satan's Downfall* (Grand Rapids, Mich.: Eerdmans, 1981), pp. 81-90. See also Walter Wink, *Naming the Powers* (Philadelphia: Fortress Press, 1984).

[6]For a practical treatment of wrestling with heavenly and earthly powers, see Michael Cassidy, *The Passing Summer* (London: Hodder and Stoughton, 1989).

[7]C. Peter Wagner, *How to Have a Healing Ministry* (Ventura, Calif.: Regal Books, 1988), pp. 196-205.

[8]Quoted in "Watchmen for the Nation," December 1989, Box 8249 Burnaby, B.C., Canada, V5C 5P8.

[9]John Dawson, *Taking Our Cities for God* (Lake Mary, Fla.: Creation House, 1989).

[10]Ibid., p. 137.

[11]Ibid., p. 41.

[12]This and the following paragraphs are a summary of John Wimber's teaching, given at his "Teach Us to Pray" seminar in San Diego, Calif., September 1984.

[13]Barth, *Ephesians 4—6,* p. 765.

[14]The absence of the definite article seems to make this point. Stott argues, however, that both truthfulness and doctrinal truth are meant. See Stott, *The Message of Ephesians,* p. 277.

[15]John Naisbitt and Patricia Aburdene, *Megatrends 2000* (New York: William Morrow and Company, 1990), pp. 270-97.

[16]Charismatics make much over the use of the term *rhema* versus *logos.* The distinction is between a specific word from the Holy Spirit and a scriptural word. This distinction is artificial and cannot be maintained with any consistency in the New Testament. However, the principle of a specific word for a specific person can be maintained. Charles Farah speaks to the issue in his *From the Pinnacle of the Temple* (Plainfield, N.J.: Logos, 1979).

[17]Simon Tugwell, *Did You Receive the Spirit?* (London: Darton, Longman & Todd, 1972), p. 17.

[18]Catherine Marshall, *Adventures in Prayer* (Old Tappan, N.J.: Revell, 1975), p. 1.

[19]Michael Green, *I Believe in the Holy Spirit* (Grand Rapids, Mich.: Eerdmans, 1975), pp. 96-98.

[20]This gift is not to be associated with the Pentecostal teaching that speaking in tongues is the initial evidence of the Spirit's presence.

Chapter 3: The Victory Is Sure

[1]"Christians Still Being Martyred," *Dallas Morning News,* June 3, 1989, p. 43A.

[2]I think this is the case with Rebecca Brown's *He Came to Set the Captives Free* (Chino, Calif.: Chick Publications, 1986).

[3]Graham Powell, *Christian Set Yourself Free* (Altona, Manitoba: Friesen Printers, 1983), p. 72.

Chapter 4: Suffering and Persecution

[1]*Those Controversial Gifts* was published by InterVarsity Press in 1983 and is now available from Grace Vineyard, Box 121012, Arlington, Texas 76012.

[2]See Ken Blue, *Authority to Heal* (Downers Grove, Ill.: InterVarsity Press, 1987), and John Wimber and Kevin Springer, *Power Healing* (San Francisco: Harper & Row, 1987), for a theology and practice of healing.

[3]This is the conclusion of New Testament scholar Peter Davids. Peter has permitted me to quote freely from some of his early research. His final statement is found in *First Epistle of Peter,* New International Commentary on the New Testament (Grand Rapids, Mich.: Eerdmans, 1990), pp. 30-44.

[4]Ralph Martin, *2 Corinthians,* Word Biblical Commentary (Waco, Tex.: Word Books, 1986), p. 415.

[5]John R. W. Stott, *The Message of the Sermon on the Mount* (Downers Grove, Ill.: InterVarsity Press, 1978), p. 33.

[6]William Hendriksen, *The Gospel of Matthew* (Grand Rapids, Mich.: Baker, 1973), p. 265.

[7]See John Stott's comments in *Evangelical Preaching: An Anthology of Sermons by Charles Simeon* (Portland, Ore.: Multnomah Press, 1986), pp. xxx-xxxii.

[8]Randy Frame, "Three Professors Part Paths with Dallas," *Christianity Today,* February 5, 1988, pp. 52-53.

[9]J. Norval Geldenhuys, *Luke,* New International Commentary on the New Testament (Grand Rapids, Mich.: Eerdmans, 1972), p. 535.

Chapter 5: Trials and Temptations

[1]James Houston, *The Transforming Friendship* (Oxford: Lion Publishing, 1989), p. 188.

[2]Walter Hilton, *Toward a Perfect Love* (Portland, Ore.: Multnomah Press), p. 51.

[3]This is the helpful thesis of David Pawson's, found in *The Normal Christian Birth* (London: Hodder and Stoughton, 1989).

[4]John R. W. Stott, *Men Made New* (Downers Grove, Ill.: InterVarsity Press, 1966), p. 91.

Chapter 6: Twentieth-Century Ghostbusters

[1]Merrill F. Unger, *Biblical Demonology* (Wheaton, Ill: Scripture Press, 1952).

[2]Paul lists the *word of knowledge* as one of the gifts of the Holy Spirit (1 Cor 12:8). As it is practiced in the church today, it refers to revelation given by the Holy Spirit about people, places and events.

[3]Some of the exegetical insights and most of the practical advice for this chapter come from training seminars of Vineyard Christian Fellowship churches.

[4]As Jonathan Edwards has observed, however, such demonstrations do not necessarily mean anything spiritual is going on. See John White's *When the Spirit Comes with Power* (Downers Grove, Ill.: InterVarsity Press, 1988).

[5]Francis MacNutt, *Healing* (Notre Dame, Ind.: Ave Maria Press, 1974), pp. 215-16.

[6]For a discussion on both sides of the issue, see C. Fred Dickason, *Demon Possession and*

the *Christian* (Chicago: Moody Press, 1987).

[7]Kenneth McAll, *Healing the Family Tree* (London: Sheldon Press, 1982), pp. 16-17.

[8]This chart was designed by John Wimber and used in his classes at Fuller Seminary.

[9]The imperfect verb used here suggests Jesus commanded the demon over and over.

[10]"Demon-expulser" is John Wimber's phrase.

[11]Matthew and Dennis Linn, *Deliverance Prayer* (New York: Paulist Press, 1981). Their practical advice on the deliverance ministry is very helpful.

Chapter 8: Enemies of Unity

[1]David B. Barrett, *World Christian Encyclopedia* (Oxford: Oxford University Press, 1982), p. 3.

[2]Peter H. Davids, *James,* New International Greek Testament Commentary (Grand Rapids, Mich.: Eerdmans, 1982), p. 151.

[3]Ibid.

Chapter 9: Beware of False Prophets

[1]David C. Aune, *Prophecy in Early Christianity and the Ancient Mediterranean World* (Grand Rapids, Mich.: Eerdmans, 1983), p. 189.

[2]Gerhard Friedrich, "προφήτης κτλ.," *Theological Dictionary of the New Testament,* ed. Gerhard Kittel and Gerhard Friedrich, trans. Geoffrey W. Bromiley, 10 vols. (Grand Rapids, Mich.: Eerdmans, 1964-76), 6:849.

[3]Wayne Grudem, *The Gift of Prophecy: In the New Testament and Today* (Westchester, Ill.: Crossway Books, 1988), pp. 17-23.

[4]Ibid., pp. 25-65.

[5]Aune, *Prophecy,* p. 47.

[6]Ibid., p. 220.

[7]James D. G. Dunn, "According to the Spirit of Jesus," *Theological Renewal* 5 (February-March 1977):18.

[8]Bruce Yocum, *Prophecy* (Ann Arbor, Mich.: Word of Life, 1976), p. 63.

[9]Bill Hamon, *Prophets and Personal Prophecy* (Shippenburg, Pa.: Destiny Image, 1987), pp. 117-30.

Chapter 11: Eleven O'Clock Demons

[1]Francis I. Andersen, *Job,* Tyndale Old Testament Commentaries (Downers Grove, Ill.: InterVarsity Press, 1976), p. 85.

Chapter 12: Thank You, Jonathan Edwards

[1]Jonathan Edwards, "The Distinguishing Marks of a Work of the Spirit of God," *The Works of Jonathan Edwards,* vol. 2 (Edinburgh: Banner of Truth, 1974), pp. 259-77.

[2]Richard F. Lovelace, *Dynamics of Spiritual Life* (Downers Grove, Ill.: InterVarsity Press, 1979), p. 41.

[3]F. F. Bruce, *The Book of Acts,* New International Commentary on the New Testament (Grand Rapids, Mich.: Eerdmans, 1971), p. 99.
[4]For an explanation of the "paradigm shift," see Charles H. Kraft, *Christianity with Power* (Ann Arbor, Mich.: Servant Publications, 1989).
[5]As quoted in David Watson's *Called and Committed* (Wheaton, Ill.: Harold Shaw, 1982), p. 189.

Chapter 13: Give the Boy a Second Chance!
[1]Loren Cunningham, *Is That Really You, God?* (Grand Rapids, Mich.: Chosen Books, 1984).
[2]For insight into this process, see Gordon MacDonald's *Rebuilding Your Broken World* (Nashville: Thomas Nelson, 1988).

Chapter 14: Glory, Sex and Money
[1]Richard Baxter, *The Reformed Pastor* (Portland, Ore.: Multnomah Press, 1982), p. 49.
[2]Leon Morris, *First and Second Epistles to the Thessalonians,* New International Commentary on the New Testament (Grand Rapids, Mich.: Eerdmans, 1973), p. 121.
[3]For a similar list and provoking article, see "The War Within: An Anatomy of Lust," name withheld, *Leadership* 3, no. 4 (Fall 1982):30-48.

Chapter 15: Trouble at the Wall
[1]John White observes some of the same ingredients, but develops a leadership theme in *Excellence in Leadership* (Downers Grove, Ill.: InterVarsity Press, 1986).
[2]As quoted by Ben Patterson, "A Small Pump at the Edge of the Swamp," *Leadership* 1, no. 2 (Spring 1980):41.